CURRENT STRATEGIES FOR TEACHERS

GOODYEAR EDUCATION SERIES
Theodore W. Hipple, Editor

CHANGE FOR CHILDREN
Sandra Nina Kaplan, Jo Ann Butom Kaplan, Sheila Kunishima Madsen, Bette K. Taylor

CRUCIAL ISSUES IN CONTEMPORARY EDUCATION
Theodore W. Hipple

CURRENT STRATEGIES FOR TEACHERS: A RESOURCE FOR PERSONALIZING INSTRUCTION
Robert L. Gilstrap and William R. Martin

EARLY CHILDHOOD EDUCATION
Marjorie Hipple

ELEMENTARY SCHOOL TEACHING: PROBLEMS AND METHODS
Margaret Kelly Giblin

FACILITATIVE TEACHING: THEORY AND PRACTICE
Robert Myrick and Joe Wittmer

THE FOUR FACES OF TEACHING
Dorothy I. Seaberg

THE FUTURE OF EDUCATION
Theodore W. Hipple

MASTERING CLASSROOM COMMUNICATION
Dorothy Grant Hennings

THE OTHER SIDE OF THE REPORT CARD
Larry Chase

POPULAR MEDIA AND THE TEACHING OF ENGLISH
Thomas R. Giblin

RACE AND POLITICS IN SCHOOL/COMMUNITY ORGANIZATIONS
Allan C. Ornstein

REFORMING METROPOLITAN SCHOOLS
Allan Ornstein, Daniel Levine, Doxey Wilkerson

SCHOOL COUNSELING: PROBLEMS AND METHODS
Robert Myrick and Joe Wittmer

SECONDARY SCHOOL TEACHING: PROBLEMS AND METHODS
Theodore W. Hipple

SOLVING TEACHING PROBLEMS
Mildred Bluming and Myron Dembo

TEACHING, LOVING, AND SELF-DIRECTED LEARNING
David Thatcher

VALUE CLARIFICATION IN THE CLASSROOM: A PRIMER
Doyle Casteel and Robert Stahl

WILL THE REAL TEACHER PLEASE STAND UP?
Mary Greer and Bonnie Rubinstein

SOCIAL STUDIES AS CONTROVERSY
R. Jerrald Shive

A YOUNG CHILD EXPERIENCES
Sandra Nina Kaplan, Jo Ann Butom Kaplan, Sheila Kunishima Madsen, Bette Taylor Gould

CURRENT STRATEGIES FOR TEACHERS:
A Resource for Personalizing Instruction

Robert L. Gilstrap
*Associate Professor of Early Childhood
and Elementary Education*

George Mason University
Fairfax, Virginia

William R. Martin
*Associate Professor
of Secondary Education*

Goodyear Publishing Company, Inc.
Pacific Palisades, California

Library of Congress Cataloging in Publication Data

Gilstrap, Robert.   Current strategies for teachers.

(Goodyear education series)
Bibliography: p.
1. Teaching.   I. Martin, William Reed, 1934-   joint author.   II. Title.
LB1025.2.G54   371.102   74-18750
ISBN 0-87620-201-6

Copyright © 1975
by Goodyear Publishing Company, Inc.,
Pacific Palisades, California

All rights reserved. No part of this book may be reproduced in any form or by any means without permission in writing from the publisher.

Library of Congress Catalog Card Number: 74-18750

ISBN: 0-87620-201-6

Y-2016-7

Current Printing (last number):
10 9 8 7 6 5 4 3 2

Printed in the United States of America

To Our Wives and Children . . .

Acknowledgments

In writing this book, we are basically optimists, believers that the human condition can be improved through education, and that education can be facilitated by skilled teaching. To our teachers, all of them, both professional and personal, we give our thanks.

We appreciate the help we received at the libraries of Montgomery County, Maryland, George Mason University, and the Curriculum Laboratory of the College of Education at the University of Maryland. The staff and consultants of Goodyear Publishing Company also provided valuable assistance. We further appreciate the help and inspiration provided by our students and colleagues at George Mason University.

We are responsible for the artwork, and overall content and organization of the book. Typing of the original manuscript was done by Deborah Kuhar. Hopefully, our efforts will help others at least as much as they have helped us.

Contents

Introduction   1

strategy 1   Lecture   7
The teacher-talk strategy; a time-honored method that has a place in the modern curriculum.
Competency Worksheet 8
Some Advantages 9
Some Disadvantages 10
Classroom Example (Elementary) 10
    Analysis/Comment 11
Classroom Example (Secondary) 11
    Analysis/Comment 12

strategy 2   Discussion   15
Students can profit from contact with the thinking of teachers as well as with that of other students. This method helps teachers provide for both.
Competency Worksheet 16
Some Advantages 18
Some Disadvantages 18
Classroom Example (Elementary) 19
    Analysis/Comment 20
Classroom Example (Secondary) 20
    Analysis/Comment 22

strategy 3   Drill and Practice   25
This well-known method to insure specific instructional outcomes is updated to employ teacher creativity and obtain increasing student interest and enjoyment.
Competency Worksheet 26
Some Advantages 27
Some Disadvantages 28
Classroom Example (Elementary) 28
    Analysis/Comment 29
Classroom Example (Secondary) 29
    Analysis/Comment 30

strategy 4   Independent Study   33
A major strategy for individualizing instruction that encourages full use of a variety of learning environments.
Competency Worksheet 34
Some Advantages 35
Some Disadvantages 36
Classroom Example (Elementary) 36
    Analysis/Comment 37
Classroom Example (Secondary) 38
    Analysis/Comment 39

strategy 5   Group Investigation   43
Student committees are helped to work on various aspects of a total group or class study to increase their competencies in group and research skills.
Competency Worksheet 44
Some Advantages 45
Some Disadvantages 46
Classroom Example (Elementary) 46
    Analysis/Comment 46
Classroom Example (Secondary) 47
    Analysis/Comment 48

strategy 6   **Laboratory Approach**   **53**

This instructional strategy provides opportunities for individuals to manipulate materials and explore environments that will increase their understandings and skills in specific content areas.

Competency Worksheet 54
Some Advantages 56
Some Disadvantages 56
Classroom Example (Elementary) 56
    Analysis/Comment 58
Classroom Example (Secondary) 59
    Analysis/Comment 60

strategy 7   **Discovery**   **63**

Instruction through guided and unguided discovery can contribute to students' analyzing and extending their abilities to solve problems through individual and group inquiry.

Competency Worksheet 64
Some Advantages 67
Some Disadvantages 68
Classroom Example (Elementary) 68
    Analysis/Comment 68
Classroom Example (Secondary) 69
    Analysis/Comment 73

strategy 8   **The Learning Center**   **77**

Discusses the strategy for providing instructional display areas where educational tasks are organized for the learner with specific objectives in mind, along with established procedures for evaluation.

Competency Worksheet 78
Some Advantages 80
Some Disadvantages 81
Classroom Example (Elementary) 81
    Analysis/Comment 81
Classroom Example (Secondary) 82
    Analysis/Comment 83

strategy 9   **Simulation**   **87**

Teachers learn to conduct problem situations and/or games for students in which pupils play roles and respond to relevant but "safe" situations with an eye toward subsequent transfer of learning.

Competency Worksheet 88
Some Advantages 89
Some Disadvantages 89
Classroom Example (Elementary) 90
    Analysis/Comment 90
Classroom Example (Secondary) 91
    Analysis/Comment 92

strategy 10   **Behavior Modification**   **95**

An approach for altering behaviors of students that will assist them in being more productive and self-directed individuals.

Competency Worksheet 96
Some Advantages 99
Some Disadvantages 99
Classroom Example (Elementary) 100
    Analysis/Comment 100
Classroom Example (Secondary) 102
    Analysis/Comment 104

strategy 11   **Performance-Based Learning Activity Package**   **109**

Learning activity packages are provided for students as part of the teacher's design to achieve predetermined learning outcomes through appropriately planned individualization of instruction.

Competency Worksheet 111
Some Advantages 112
Some Disadvantages 113
Classroom Example
   (Elementary and Secondary) 113
    Analysis/Comment 118

strategy 12   **Do-Look-Learn**   **121**

A teaching method that starts with pupil involvement, continues through emphasis on process as well as product, and, hopefully, never really ends for students.

Competency Worksheet 122
Some Advantages 123
Some Disadvantages 124
Classroom Example (Elementary) 124
    Analysis/Comment 125
Classroom Example (Secondary) 126
    Analysis/Comment 127

An Annotated List of Selected Resources for Further Study   **129**

CURRENT STRATEGIES FOR TEACHERS

Introduction

The continuing search to find ways of personalizing instruction—a characteristic of the current scene in American education—is the recurring theme of this book. We believe that when teachers possess a repertoire of teaching skills and behaviors—in a word, *strategies*—they are better able to help students attain instructional objectives in ways best for each individual. With *Current Strategies for Teachers*, we attempt to help teachers and future teachers in their quest for a more personalized education for those they teach.

The dozen strategies are offered in a generally chronological order. In all cases, we believe that enough information is provided in this book for college students and teachers who wish to teach through a strategy to be able to do so. The reader is encouraged to begin with any strategy that appeals to his particular interest or need and to skip back and forth as desired. All are representative of current major modes and practices of educational thought, and of models that are being used by the American teacher. Interestingly enough, in researching the book we found that some of the relatively exotic-sounding methods, such as Sylvia Ashton Warner's "organic method of teaching" and Maria Montessori's "sensory learning method," are taken in under one or more of the more generally familiar designations as "discovery," "laboratory approach," or "group investigation." We have elected to stay with these more inclusive categories.

In addition, we realize that for any single learning experience, competent teachers might combine a number of strategies to provide for individual differences. Our attempt is not to suggest that the strategies be used in an isolated manner, but rather to help make teachers increasingly aware of what they are doing in terms of their instructional methods and of what they might do.

All the current teaching strategies selected meet the formal definition of a strategy that we used as a criterion:

> Patterns of teacher behavior that are recurrent, applicable to various subject matters, characteristic of more than one teacher, and relevant to learning.[1]

This eliminates for us such "methods" as *brainstorming, guest speakers, psychodrama, filmstrips,* and the like. These we would consider as skills, tactics, or materials that might well be involved as a part of a teaching strategy.

Each strategy discussed has its own background section. Each background offers some information on the roots or origins of the strategy, based upon the professional thinking most closely associated with the strategy. Further, the background section provides a general picture of the use of the strategy in American schools today, along with research findings in regard to the strategy. Research, by the way, is inconclusive on methods of teaching, although educators agree that "there is no one best teaching method that fits all situations."[2] Finally, we offer in the background, the purposes of the strategy as well as a definition. Unless otherwise indicated, we have drawn our definitions from the standard reference *Dictionary of Education*, in an effort to be precise in an area in which confusion of terminology abounds.

The background section in each strategy is followed by perhaps the single most important item in *Current Strategies For Teachers:* a competency worksheet for planning and observing. The worksheet consists of a list of checkpoints of the observable behaviors that usually comprise the strategy, as well as a place for observer's notes. We believe the checkpoints reflect the major behaviors and procedures a teacher would use to implement the strategy for successfully facilitating student learning. (Generally, we should note, we have used "he" to refer to an individual teacher or student. We recognize the equality of "she," but were unable to find a suitable word that is widely enough accepted at the present time to serve for both sexes.)

Each worksheet has its checkpoint items arranged in a quasi-chronological order; that is, basically in the order of occurrence, as a teacher would use the strategy in the classroom. From our point of view, the checkpoints are appropriately thought of as guides to the observable behavior of a teacher as he or she implements a particular strategy in the classroom. Some of the listed behaviors may seem to the reader to include more than what may be observed in a classroom during one lesson. In addition, some of the checkpoint items are characteristic of more than one strategy.

On the whole, the competency worksheets for planning and observing may be used, as desired, in connection with such materials as videotape playback, supervisor's reports, and teacher-teacher feedback. For example, in-service teachers might establish with colleagues a reciprocal agreement wherein each sits in on the other's class and records data that can be given through the applied worksheet to the person instructing. Because no value judgments are required, unless requested by the person being observed, the experience can be revealing and non-threatening in giving a teacher a picture of himself as he sees how adequately he performs a particular sequence for instruction. On the basis of this, modification is feasible if desired by the teacher. That is to say, the checkpoint part of each competency worksheet is meant to describe, not prescribe. Nonetheless, it can be used by a teacher for bringing about changes in his own behavior. The checkpoint part of the competency worksheet might also be used, for example, to help a teacher or teacher-in-training plan or evaluate a learning experience for students. Moreover, the checkpoints can be used for observing the listed teacher behaviors "live" or from film or tape. The space provided for notes will aid in this usage.

After each competency worksheet, we have provided some advantages and disadvantages of each strategy. These, like the worksheets themselves, represent a cumulation of thought from our readings, interviews with teachers, observations in classrooms, and professional teaching experience. We have tried to be objective in recording the advantages and disadvantages, so that they would reflect what educators believe about the strategies rather than being strictly our own opinions. Study of the disadvantages, for instance, might actually encourage the use of a strategy if the deficiencies can be viewed as being relatively easy to work out.

Next, from our reading and experience, we have offered classroom examples of each strategy in operation at the elementary and the secondary level. These are representative of a variety of curriculum areas and offer a kind of simulated observation in which the reader is invited to join us. In the analysis/comment section that follows each example, we have chosen to review the use of the strategy as it occurred in the example. We do this as if the reader were in a position to talk with us, in terms especially of the checkpoints, about what has just taken place in the example.

After the introduction and the strategies themselves, the last major section in the book is what we call "An Annotated List of Selected Resources." Here we have named and briefly described sample materials that we recommend, from our professional experience, for use with the strategies in grades K-12. Each strategy dis-

INTRODUCTION

cussed in the book is listed at the end of the book with a number of resources. Criteria we used for including materials were as follows:

> Is the item helpful, in itself, for teachers desiring to teach through the strategy under which it is to be listed?
>
> Is the item useful as a reminder of other materials and types of materials that teachers could use in implementing a certain strategy?
>
> Is the item applicable to at least common teaching-learning areas such as science, math, modern foreign languages, history, and English?
>
> Is the item fairly recently published and readily accessible?
>
> Does it actually represent the strategy as described in our book?
>
> Is the item interesting and worthwhile (in our subjective opinion)?

The resources list—though certainly not inclusive—should serve as a beginning on which persons interested in one or more of the strategies might build.

To be sure, each strategy on which we report could be discussed in a full book or more. We have tried to be concise but not misleading.

It might help the reader, at this point, if we mention a number of areas relating to instructional strategies that have not been dealt with in this book. Some that might be recognized include a detailed review of research findings on the various strategies in terms of their effects on student learning for application, transfer, and retention; a study of the conceptualized models for moving toward a theory of instruction out of which teaching methods evolve; and a review of the various ways of classifying approaches to teaching methods. Our way basically reflects the generally accepted viewpoint of instructional strategies as being on a continuum from expository (directive) to heuristic (non-directive), or from methods in which the student is a recipient of knowledge to methods in which the student finds out for himself. No attempt has been made to provide an inclusive bibliography. Some books that do this kind of job are available (the reader must make the connections to particular strategies). One, for instance, is the National Council of Teachers of English publication *Guide to Teaching Materials For English*, Grades 7-12.

What we do offer is a practical beginning for inexperienced as well as experienced teachers. With it, the teacher can check what he is doing or could be doing with regard to instructional strategies in common use today.

With these components made available, we believe the book can help in several important ways. For one thing, it can contribute to the study of teaching. Those who think through and make use of the information, competency worksheets, classroom examples, and references contained herein should gain an increased understanding of a variety of instructional techniques. Moreover, if teaching is an art grounded in skill, as we believe it is, the teacher who wants to be truly a professional in the classroom will benefit from reviewing the basic behaviors of his own teaching strategies. We see the book, then, as providing a resource for teachers—and for those preparing to be teachers—to use in analyzing the number and effectiveness of their own strategies of teaching. Teachers working with the book may find it helpful in adding further strategies, or in modifying ones presently used, to personalize instruction for their students.

Besides making a contribution to the study of teaching and, of course, to elementary and secondary teaching specifically, what is provided here is meant also to serve persons working in a helping relationship with those charged with teaching elementary and secondary students. College-level instructors of methods courses and the like might find the introductions, competency worksheets, and selected resources especially helpful, for example, in aiding pre-professionals to discover new knowlege and to think objectively about a major component of the teaching act—the strategy of the teacher.

Teachers of teachers might also raise questions like the following with their undergraduate or graduate students, using the book when helpful: What constitutes an instructional strategy? By what criteria of professional decision making is a strategy selected for use? What are some of the available models for instruction? How is the instructional strategy a part of the larger process of teaching? What teaching pattern is being followed by a teacher being observed? Is the instructional strategy as complete as it might be? What current curriculum materials making use of the different strategies are available? Where can one turn to find out more about teaching strategies and the research that supports them? Questions like these and others can stimulate discussion and growth in classes of teachers. In addition, supervisors of both student teachers and in-service teachers might find the competency worksheets particularly valuable in counseling. With objective data before them, both "helper" and "helpee" can interact more effectively and productively with regard to what did or did not occur in the classroom and to what might be done to modify a particular teaching technique in subsequent teaching efforts.

Finally, we would be remiss if we did not also offer our rationale as to *why* we have written *Current Strategies for Teachers*.

Our strong contention is that most teachers are made, not born. A part of their professional growth for which they may justly be held accountable involves attaining a number of ways to help students interact with the designated curriculum in order to make learning the most productive experience possible. Knowledge of and ability to apply the variety of ways, patterns, or teaching strategies on the current scene is one of the crucial distinguishing differences between the layman and the professional teacher. Within the profession, possession of a repertoire of strategies is a measure of competency that helps to separate the master teacher from his more limited colleagues.

We write, then, from an awareness of what research says, in general, about instructional methods and from our own thinking, to aid those who wish to be master teachers—those who realize the necessity for continually studying teaching and for having at their conscious command an increasing number of strategies for interacting with different students to achieve different objectives in ways best for these students. (The opposite type of teacher has been referred to by Dwight Allen, Dean of the School of Education, University of Massachusetts. He is generally given credit for saying that the teacher who has only one strategy can be replaced with a machine and should be!)

As to a final comment on why this book was written, suffice it to say that we believe the self-fulfillment of the human being, and thereby the improvement of society itself, can be aided through education. Competence in a variety of strategies gives the teacher maximum chance to affect changes in human behavior that are both necessary and desirable if we are to have intelligent, sensitive, articulate persons to cope with and lead a society beset with complex problems and challenges. If this book can help—if, in fact, it can contribute to a teacher's instructional repertoire and to his analysis thereof, and perhaps just a little to the self-actualization of the individuals with whom the teacher comes into professional contact—it will have met our purpose.

NOTES

1. Robert L. Ebel (ed.), *Encyclopedia of Educational Research* (4th ed., New York: Macmillan Co., 1969), p. 1446.

2. Dwight W. Allen and Eli Seifman (eds.), *The Teacher's Handbook* (Glenview, Illinois: Scott, Foresman and Company, 1971), p. 61.

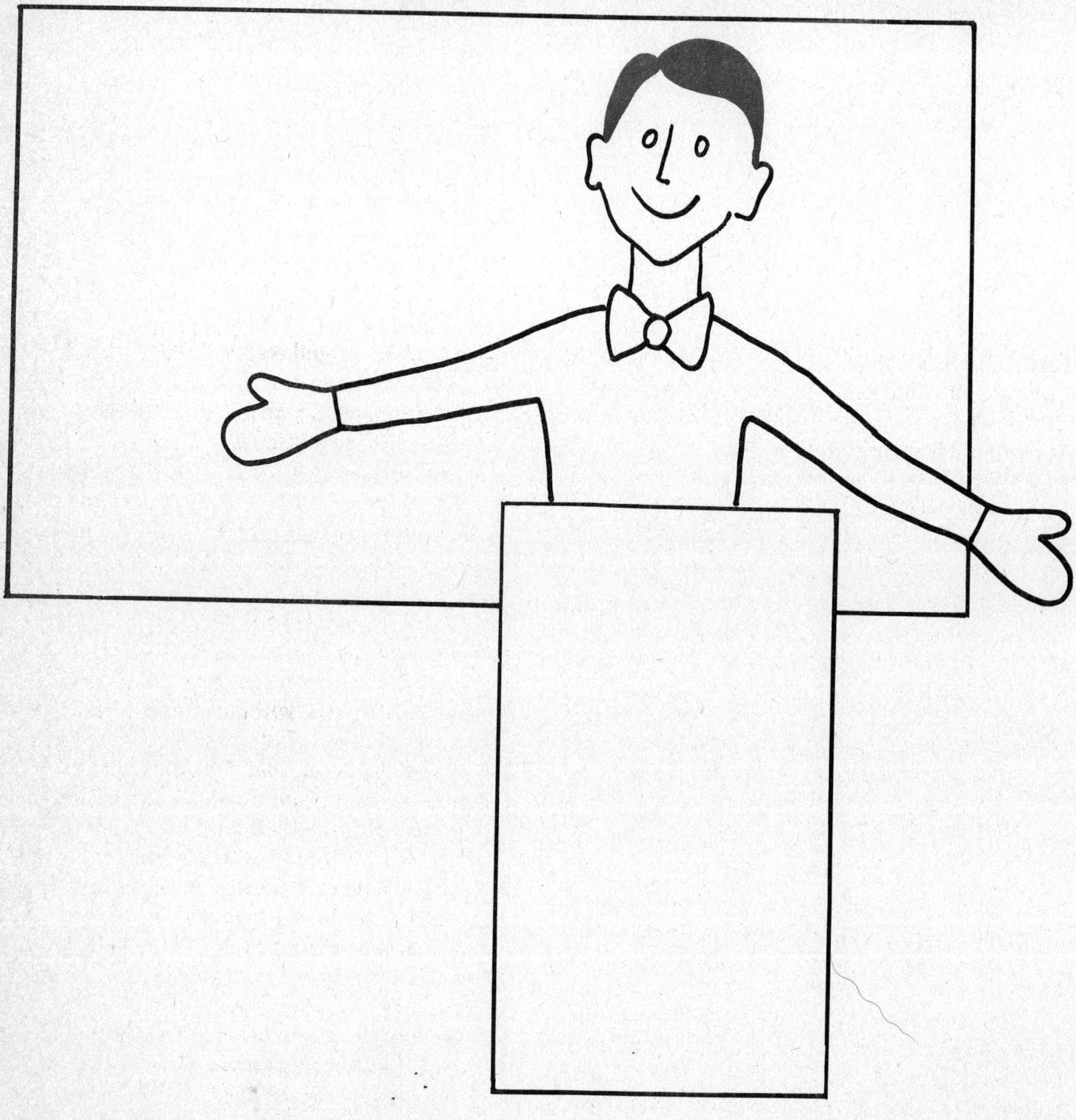

strategy 1

Lecture

BACKGROUND

Contrast Mr. Thomas Gradgrind, as described by Charles Dickens, and Melvin Heller, author of "Learning Through Lectures," in their pedagogical advice, and one gets some idea of the range for the lecture method:

Hard Times

Teach these boys and girls nothing but Facts. Facts alone are wanted in life. Plant nothing else, and root out everything else. You can only form the minds of reasoning animals upon Facts: nothing else will ever be of any service to them. This is the principle on which I bring up my own children, and this is the principle on which I bring up these children. Stick to Facts, Sir![1]

"Learning Through Lectures"

Lecture can challenge the imagination of each student, arouse curiosity, develop his spirit of inquiry, and encourage his creativity.[2]

The lecture method, which shows such disparity, was in use for instructional purposes long before the time of Christ. Later, in the second half of the fifth century, the ancient Greek Sophists saw and used lecture as a carefully thought-out discourse or a brilliant improvisation on some theme or other. The word "lecture" itself derives from the Latin word *lego (legere, lectus)* which means "to read." Before the invention of the printing press, those fortunate enough to possess a book would read aloud while students listened and took notes. Times, it would seem, changed more rapidly than did instructional procedures; teachers continued to base instruction on readings from text materials long after books became available to all. And, soon, *lego* became generalized to mean "to teach," and the dictation type of instruction became labeled, and often libeled, as the "lecture method."

In its modern version, it is true that the method has been abused. As has been said, the words of the teacher quite often *do* go into the notes of the student without passing through the minds of either. We would agree with Ausubel's claim, however, that "the weaknesses attributed to the method of verbal instruction do not inhere in the method itself."[3] The faults, such as they are, reside in the practitioner. The primary question for those planning to use the lecture method should center not on the so-called faults or abuses of lecture, however, but on the objectives for which it is to be used and on the ways in which it is more or less effective in achieving these objectives than are other methods for the individual students involved.

Although research has failed to make a favorable case for any superiority of the lecture method over other instructional strategies, its use as a method for personalizing instruction in K-12 does depend on who uses it, on the nature of the experiences afforded students, and on the kinds of learning outcomes sought.[4] Further, we can say from our own experience that a teacher's purpose in lecturing should be along the lines of giving instructions, clarifying an issue, sharing a pertinent personal experience, or utilizing his expertise to expand student knowledge beyond readily available resources. The current definition of modern lecturing is a method of teaching by which the teacher gives an oral presentation of facts or principles.

The user of lecture, then, needs to both cope with the limitations of the method and utilize its strengths to his best advantage. For in this way, communication of knowledge through verbal exposition can be meaningful to students, and the tradition of the lecture need no longer be subjected to unexamined criticism.

COMPETENCY WORKSHEET FOR PLANNING AND OBSERVING

Checkpoints

Observer Notes

When using the lecture strategy, the teacher is usually observed performing the following behaviors:

_____ Obtaining the attention of the audience at the start.

_____ Making clear the purpose of the lecture.

_____ Indicating the point of view from which the subject is to be presented.

_____ Making checks to determine where the listeners "are" in regard to the material presented.

_____ Defining the time limit in advance for the students.

_____ Connecting the lecture to prelecture learning.

_____ Following an observable organizational pattern; e.g., 20 percent (telling what will be told); 60 percent (telling); 20 percent (telling what was told).

_____ Accompanying the lecture with multisensory aids.

_____ Talking with sufficient volume to reach all listeners.

_____ Projecting warmth, friendliness, confidence, and interest in the subject.

LECTURE

_____ Providing for repetition of main ideas.

_____ Varying stress and intonation.

_____ Providing variety in pacing of ideas and verbal delivery.

_____ Indicating the relationship of one subtopic to another.

_____ Incorporating figures of speech to facilitate understanding and/or to define terms.

_____ Incorporating examples.

_____ Using humor to relieve tension, refocus attention, and create more of a mutual bond.

_____ Using nonverbal communication that is in agreement with verbal.

_____ Highlighting main ideas verbally; e.g., so students may take notes.

_____ Allowing for audience feedback through paraphrases and questions.

SOME ADVANTAGES

The following are often mentioned as some of the advantages of the lecture strategy:

- It is economical with classroom time, because it brings the teacher's ideas into immediate focus.

- It allows the teacher to use his experience, knowledge, and wisdom rather than relying only on methods that cause the students to struggle for themselves by trial and error. For example, the lecturer's experience can show students an exact relationship to be studied and can help them to by-pass unimportant details.

- The method permits the teacher to cope with large numbers of students and, when necessary, to cover a large amount of material.

- It helps students develop ability to listen accurately, critically, and with appreciation.

- It can provide exposure to knowledge not readily found in assigned readings or the common experience of the students.

- If the right "personality" is lecturing, the method can be unusually stimulating and can enhance student desire to learn in the academic area.

- The strategy is helpful for introducing a new topic of study by providing background material that students will need to prepare them for further study.

- It earns further status for the teacher by allowing him to reveal his knowledge of the subject to students.

- It permits variations with team work, mini-lectures, and small group follow-up, which can contribute to student learning from the lecture itself. For example, two teachers could alternate in giving a lecture, much like a news broadcast team, and could follow this with division of students into two groups, with each teacher leading one group for discussion of the lecture topic.

- The strategy can reinforce student readings and learnings from other sources. For example, a lecture could be given on the personal experience of "rock-hounding" while backpacking on the Appalachian Trail, which could amplify student learning from texts about the geological formation of mountains.

SOME DISADVANTAGES
The following are often mentioned as some of the disadvantages of the lecture strategy:

- It places at a disadvantage those students who have neither learned to listen nor to take notes.

- It tends to be a one-way process, with students in a passive role.

- It may cause the teacher to cover the same ground that a pupil could cover easily by a quick reading.

- It is difficult to measure student learning and/or interest (at least during the lecture).

- The strategy progresses at the pace of the speaker rather than that of the pupil.

- It can be seen as encouraging retention of facts as an end in itself; for example, a biology teacher could inform a student of so many names of body parts that the student loses interest in finding out how these parts work and why it is helpful to know them in the first place.

- The strategy tends to encourage acceptance of the teacher as final authority.

- It tends to emphasize the interests of lecturer rather than students.

- It is often inadequate for teaching skills and attitudes.

CLASSROOM EXAMPLE (ELEMENTARY)
In this elementary school, the three teachers at each grade level worked together as a team. The school was an open one, with a large space providing a work area for about ninety children. The boys and girls were working individually and in small groups when a bell rang, indicating that it was time for them to assemble as a total group in the middle of the large space facing a projection screen. It was time for social studies.

The teacher obtained the attention of the children by turning on an overhead projector that placed the words "Our Government" on the screen behind her. The children settled rather quickly. It appeared that they were anticipating something special from the teacher. When she had the attention of the group, she turned off the projector and began to explain that she wanted to talk with them today about the executive branch of the United States government, the next phase of their study.

Although the group was large, she asked for someone to tell her what branches of the government had already been discussed in their social studies class. Several children raised their hands. She called on one who reminded the class that they had already been introduced to all three branches but that the teacher had only talked about the legislative branch so far.

The teacher nodded her approval with a smile and turned on the overhead projector again. This time it projected a chart showing the three branches of government and their relationship to one another. She turned off the projector and asked someone to summarize what they had talked about concerning the legislative branch of government. This time she called on a girl who was near the back of the group. The girl mentioned the purpose of the legislative branch, how it was organized, and how the members were selected. The teacher looked pleased with the answer and asked if anyone could think of any additional information that had been shared at the large group session when she had talked with them about the legislative branch. Several hands went up, and she called on a boy who mentioned that the legislative branch must vote approval for all money that the president wants for any of his departments.

The teacher complimented the children on

how well they had reviewed what had been learned from the earlier session. She then projected on the screen a chart detailing the executive branch. She followed basically the same outline she had used for the legislative branch presentation that had been given to the large group session the day before. As she described the various cabinet positions, she used transparencies of recent newspaper clippings that revealed the executive branch in action. She suggested that the children begin to look more carefully at their daily newspapers and to clip articles that could be used on a bulletin board that was labeled "Our Government in Action."

After the teacher had completed the body of the presentation, which had been accompanied throughout with overhead transparencies, she turned off the projector and asked the children to try to summarize what they had learned today by telling a person next to them at least one thing they had learned. She gave them several minutes for this type of review, and then she turned the projector back on with a transparency that said "Main Ideas" at the top. The rest of the screen was dark. She then uncovered each main idea that she had talked about, asking the children to nod if they had mentioned this in their discussion. She encouraged the children to jot these ideas down in their notebooks, for their use in locating clippings for the group bulletin board and for their independent project.

She complimented them on their good behavior and then asked the team leader to come to the front of the group and explain the next activity.

Analysis/Comment (Elementary)

This elementary teacher possessed all the needed competencies to use the lecture method well with a large group of children. She felt comfortable with the method and believed that it was the most effective one for introducing the children to the complexities of the basic organization of the United States government. She took time to set the stage for her presentation of new ideas by involving the children in a review of what had come before. If she had not received correct responses to her questions, she would undoubtedly have spent more time reviewing and attempting to clarify the ideas that she had presented the previous day.

Her use of the overhead projector was particularly impressive. She used it not only for presenting images on the screen behind her but also as a way of getting attention at the beginning of the class as well as following the "buzz session" near the end of the presentation. She also used it to project materials such as the newspaper clippings, which could not have been presented effectively to the total group in any other manner.

If you reread the Competency Worksheet for Planning and Observing, you will see that more attention was given to some items than to others. Although she was not asked, it may be assumed that this teacher did not think it necessary to remind the children that she was attempting to present objective information about the topic; they were probably not yet aware that any other than an objective point of view could be presented. She also found it unnecessary to mention the amount of time to be spent on this topic; a pattern for large group sessions had already been established in the school, and the children were well aware that approximately 30 minutes would be spent in the large group session each day.

The other two members of the teaching team also enhanced this lecture, because they casually handled the few children who did not respond well to this approach, either by reminding them of the appropriate behavior for a large group session or by making the children sit on the side next to them so that they could better control behavior.

CLASSROOM EXAMPLE (SECONDARY)

In the example that follows, Louis Sullivan, who was largely responsible for making "form follows function" the battle cry of the modern architect, gives an account of his high school "master" opening the school year 1870-71 by lecture:

> Seated at last, Louis glanced at the master, whose appearance and make-up suggested, in a measure, a farmer of the hardy, spare, weather-beaten, penurious, successful type—apparently a man of forty or under. When

silence had settled over the mob, the master rose and began an harangue to his raw recruit; indeed he plunged into it without a word of welcome. He was a man above medium height, very scant beard, shocky hair; his movements were panther-like, his features, in action, were set as with authority and pugnacity, like those of a first mate taking on a fresh crew.

He was tense, and did not swagger—a man of passion. He said, in substance: "Boys, you don't know me, but you soon will. The discipline here will be rigid. You have come here to learn and I'll see that you do. I will not only do my share but I will make you do yours. You are here under my care; no other man shall interfere with you. I rule here— I am master here—as you will soon discover. You are here as wards in my charge; I accept that charge as sacred; I accept the responsibility involved as a high, exacting duty I owe to myself and equally to you. I will give to you all that I have; you shall give to me all that you have. But mark you: The first rule of discipline shall be SILENCE. Not a desk-top shall be raised, not a book touched, no shuffling of feet, no whispering, no sloppy movements, no rustling. I do not use the rod, I believe it the instrument of barbarous minds and weak wills, but I will shake the daylight out of any boy who transgresses, after one warning. The second rule shall be STRICT ATTENTION. You are here to learn, to think, to concentrate on the matter in hand, to hold your minds steady. The third rule shall cover ALERTNESS. You shall be awake all the time—body and brain; you shall cultivate promptness, speed, nimbleness, dexterity of mind. The fourth rule: You shall learn to LISTEN; to listen in silence with the whole mind, not part of it; to listen with your whole heart, not part of it, for sound listening is a basis for sound thinking; sympathetic listening is a basis for sympathetic, worth-while, thinking; accurate listening is a basis of accurate thinking. Finally you are to learn to OBSERVE, to REFLECT, to DISCRIMINATE. But this subject is of such high importance, so much above your present understanding, that I will not comment upon it now; it is not to be approached without due preparation. I shall not start with you with a jerk, but tighten the lines bit by bit until I have you firmly in hand at the most spirited pace you can go." As he said this last saying, a dangerous smile went back and forth over his grim set face. As to the rest, he outlined the curriculum and his plan of procedure for the coming year. He stressed matters of hygiene; and stated that a raised hand would always have attention. Lessons were then marked off in the various books—all were to be "home lessons"—and the class was dismissed for the day.

Louis was amazed, thunderstruck, dumbfounded, overjoyed! He had caught and weighed every word as it fell from the lips of the master; to each thrilling word he had vibrated in open-eyed, amazed response. He knew now that through the years his thoughts, his emotions, his dreams, his feelings, his romance, his visions, had been formless and chaotic; now in this man's utterances, they were voiced in explosive condensation, in a flash they became defined, living, real. A pathway had been shown him, a wholly novel plan revealed that he grasped as a banner in his hand, as homeward bound he cried within, "At last a Man!"[5]

Analysis/Comment (Secondary)

A few points should be made about the lesson of this teacher, one Moses Woolson by name. His didactic approach is obviously appropriate for consideration as an illustration of the lecture strategy or, at least, of the lecture approach. The lecturing is done in the traditional form and yet, in this case, it seems to transcend the "horror" stories that often accrue to a teacher relying on the approach.

In terms of the checkpoints, the presentation lacks many of the "niceties" that teachers concerned with implementing this strategy should follow. No visual aids, no projection of warmth, no use of humor, no (or probably no) nonverbal emphases, and certainly no acceptance of feedback from the audience are evident, for example. On the other hand, it must be acknowledged that the attention of the audience is obtained and held and that the points mentioned are likely to be retained. Moreover, the purpose of the lecture is clear, as is the point of view from which teaching will be presented. There is little doubt as to who is in charge and for what. Further, there is no problem with volume, and the organization, relationship, and presentation of ideas are concise and vivid. The lecture, in sum, is effective; witness Louis' reaction at the end of the excerpt.

The true effectiveness of this lecture is traceable, however, not only to the application of some of the items on the checklist (probably never even considered by Mr. Woolson), but also, and perhaps more importantly, to the apparent intensity, interest, and honesty in presentation. Although not "perfect" in terms of meeting all the worksheet characteristics, this lecture is really effective through the qualities of the man himself. We hope all teachers can be as effective human beings. We hope they can also use the lecture strategy effectively as a vehicle to help some students learn some things best in this way. We would remind teachers, however, that when *skills* wittingly accompany the qualities of the person evidenced by this "Great Teacher," satisfactory results in terms of student learning are more likely to be attainable for more teachers.

NOTES

1. Charles Dickens, *Hard Times* (New York: Everyman's Library, E. P. Dutton & Co., 1966), p. 1.

2. Melvin P. Heller, "Learning Through Lectures," *Clearing House* 37 (October 1962), p. 99.

3. David P. Ausubel, "In Defense of Verbal Learning," *Educational Theory* 11 (January 1961), p. 16.

4. Chester W. Harris (ed.), *Encyclopedia of Educational Research* (3rd ed.; New York: Macmillan Co., 1960), pp. 280, 851.

5. Houston Peterson (ed.), *Great Teachers Portrayed by Those Who Studied Under Them* (New York: Vintage Books, 1946), pp. 56-58. (Copyrighted by the Trustees of Rutgers College in New Jersey and reprinted by permission of the Rutgers University Press.)

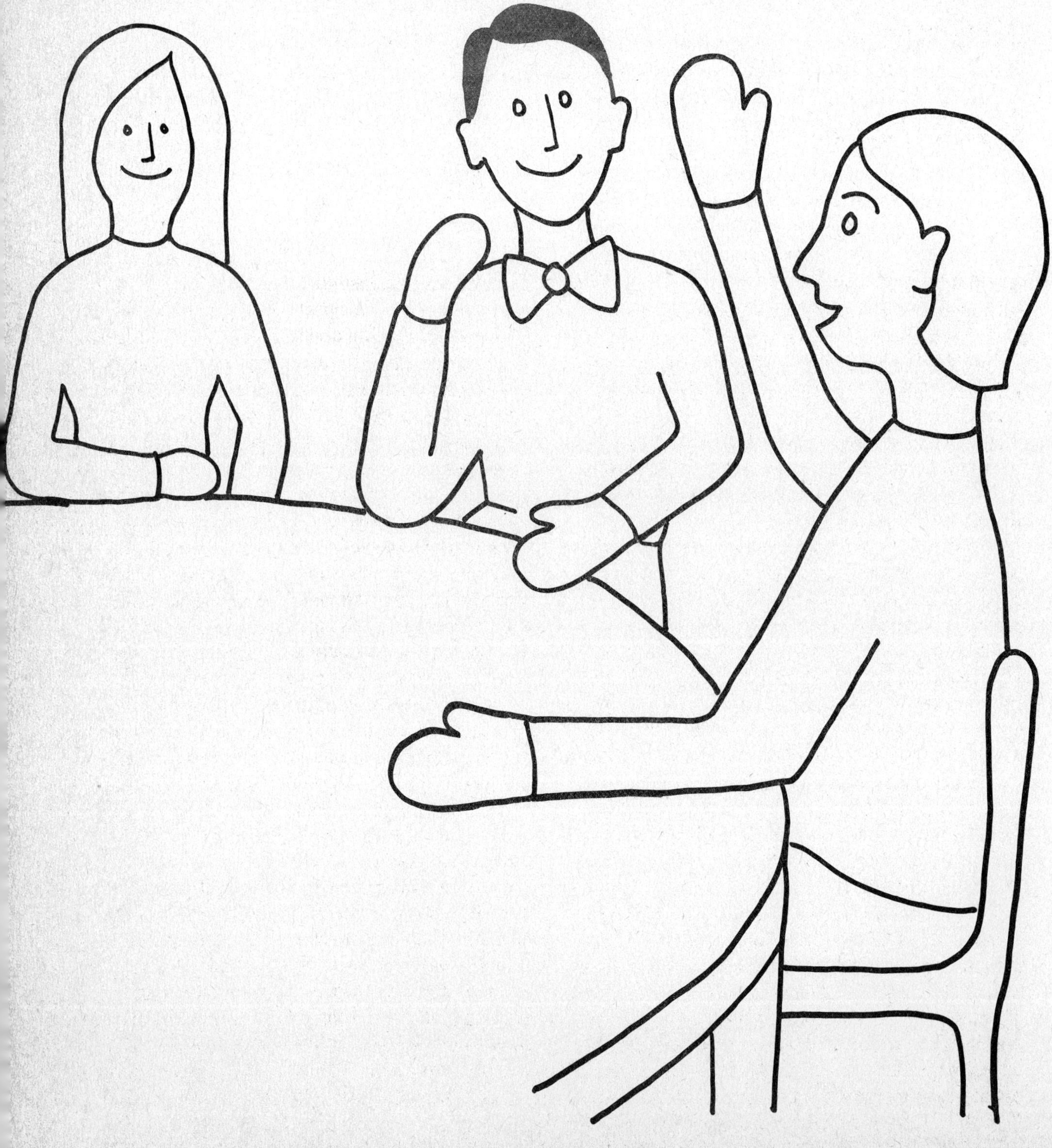

strategy 2

Discussion

BACKGROUND
Although it is most probable that people have been discussing ever since they first began to speak, it is with the early Greek and Roman civilizations that discussion seems to have initially been used as a formal method for instruction; witness Plato's notion that knowledge lies within —with the teacher serving as a kind of "midwife" whose job it is to assist at the birth of ideas in the minds of students.

In modern times, discussion has gained prominence as a function of democratic classroom procedures. It is defined as an activity in which people talk together in order to share information about a topic or problem, or to seek answers to a problem based on all possible evidence. Within this definition, various categories of discussion can be designated: whole class, small group, guided, permissive, leaderless—to name a few.

Many classroom teachers are currently using a pertinent version of the strategy that is offered by William Glasser. He has applied the psychiatric principles he calls "reality therapy" to the classroom through the basic mechanism of the *Classroom Meeting*, a 30- to 45-minute period at least once a week when students and teacher engage in open-minded, non-judgmental discussion of problems in an effort to find collective solutions. The three types of classroom meetings are, first, the social-problem-solving meeting, which is usually concerned with behavioral and social problems; in this type, the students attempt to share the responsibility for learning and behaving by resolving their problems within the classroom. Second is the open-ended meeting, in which students are asked to discuss any thought-provoking questions related to their lives, questions that may also be related to the curriculum of the classroom. And, third, the educational-diagnostic meeting is directly related to what the class is studying; its purpose is to get an idea whether the class has understood the lesson, and what members know and do not know. In all three types, the most important aspect of the classroom meeting is that it can be used to help students achieve behavioral change to the end that they will become increasingly more responsible, integrated, and responsive persons who can direct and monitor their own further growth.[1]

Our investigation of recent research reported in standard reference sources reveals several interesting points relative to discussion: One is that teachers who generally use student ideas for some periods of discussion and those who build on student ideas are teachers whose students often have, and continue to have, (1) higher-than-average achievement on tests of information; (2) positive attitudes toward school, teachers, and subject matter under study; (3) lower levels of anxiety; and (4) more positive self-concepts. Another general finding indicates that the more direct a teacher is in influencing students, the less students learn, at least in such areas of higher cognitive processes as the ability to think critically. Teacher common sense suggests that the more students contribute, the more involved they become and the more they learn. In view of these "findings," the teacher would do well to spend class time in using the discussion technique, whatever its external form. The strategy check list that follows is based primarily, but not exclusively, on Glasser's model of the Classroom Meeting. The checklist, like the method, is not sufficient in itself. If employed professionally, however, the list and its encompassing method can release in students that "energy of wanting"[2] in the pursuit of educational (and humanizing) goals that should be characteristic of all methods and, ideally, of all learners.

COMPETENCY WORKSHEET FOR PLANNING AND OBSERVING

Checkpoints

Observer Notes

When using the discussion strategy, the teacher is usually observed performing the following behaviors:

_____ Planning in advance the type of discussion; e.g., problem-solving, open-ended, educational-diagnostic.

_____ Providing an initial "jumping off" activity; e.g., a field trip, reading assignment, mutual concern.

_____ Organizing the physical facilities to enhance discussion; e.g., arranging chairs in a tight circle.

_____ Locating himself and students to facilitate discussion; e.g., the teacher may choose to sit in a different part of the circle for each discussion; he may wish to intersperse those who constantly talk to one another with other students; he may wish to move from group to group, if more than one group is operating.

_____ Providing sufficient and appropriate multi-media materials.

_____ Encouraging students to participate in responding, interacting, challenging, and, as appropriate, conducting the discussion.

DISCUSSION

_____ Referring questions back to the group or to individuals in the group.

_____ Using probing questions, especially those of the "why" and "how" type.

_____ Generally refraining from judging student answers or responses as "right" or "wrong"; i.e., accepting student opinions as being worthy of further critical thought.

_____ Being supportive; for example, by giving credit for perceptive contributions and by providing ample time for participants to develop ideas and responses.

_____ Giving help at appropriate times; e.g., by rephrasing questions for the group, by suggesting that members back up opinions, by calling for summaries or clarification when needed, and, if necessary, by asking students to raise hands to participate.

_____ Helping students make personal value judgments and commitments with regard to their own behavior; for instance, when such judgments and commitments are in accord with the teacher's objectives for the discussion.

_____ Enabling the discussion to move toward some positive end or purpose; e.g., a reasonable alternative solution to a problem.

_____ Keeping to an accepted format for the discussion; e.g., staying within a reasonable time limit, being consistent in scheduling additional dis-

_____ cussions, and including summaries.

_____ Evaluating with at least equal emphasis both what happened in the discussion and how it happened.

SOME ADVANTAGES

The following are often mentioned as some of the advantages of the discussion strategy:

- It frees the teacher to assume additional "helping" roles within the class, such as that of a silent recorder at the board or as a participant in group discussion.

- It involves students directly in the process of learning as they serve as participants, group leaders, and framers of discussion questions.

- It can provide opportunities for all students to participate, particularly if the discussion is carried on in small groups.

- It may cause participants in a discussion to gain self-confidence.

- The strategy can help an individual student see that his tentative groping on a problem, for instance, is shared by others, and it can, perhaps, enable the student and others who may share the problem achieve a more appropriate solution than they might have reached on their own.

- The pooling of the group's information may result in new insights for various members of the group.

- The method can facilitate social objectives of schooling; for example, bright students can sit with and help less able students in small groups; individual students can be brought into a discussion by the teacher as they evidence social and intellectual readiness.

- It urges students to learn and practice intellectual processes such as organizing facts, asking discerning questions, and thinking reflectively on relationships within and among personal ideas, the ideas of others, and the realities of the situation.

- The strategy can be used nicely before, during, and after other methods such as *lecture* and *discovery*.

- It provides the give-and-take necessary to help students understand and prepare for their roles as citizens in a democracy.

- It gives the teacher and students chances to attain effective interpersonal relations, through the frequent mutual practice of interpersonal communication skills in the real situations of the discussions.

- It can provide pupils with increasing amounts of intellectual independence, which would lead them away from merely reiterating the teacher's viewpoint.

- The method permits variety in usage, such as panel discussion, debate, and symposium.

- It offers each student the opportunity to test, alter, and improve views, values, and judgments that might be shown to be inadequate under the scrutiny of thoughtful group consideration.

SOME DISADVANTAGES

The following are often mentioned as some of the disadvantages of the discussion strategy:

- The strategy does not guarantee accomplishment, even if there is group agreement or consensus at the end of a session, because the decisions reached may not be implemented.

- Discussion is unpredictable, even when carefully organized; it could easily turn into an aimless "free-for-all" or go off on a tangent, particularly when student leadership is nonproductive.

- The strategy usually does not function well unless participants have a common background of knowledge.

- It requires discussion skills on the part of all participants that are needed to enhance their effective participation and that may not have been previously learned.

- It needs flexible physical arrangements and scheduling, which may not be available.

- The strategy may become "fake" if the leader has difficulties in maintaining an open mind since he knows the kind of answer he wants and will accept no others.

- It could lead to group dominance by one or several members, with the rest becoming disinterested spectators.

CLASSROOM EXAMPLE (ELEMENTARY)

When this classroom observation of eight- and nine-year-old children began, the teacher was at the front of the room near the chalkboard. The children were scattered about the room sitting at individual desks, which were arranged in groups of four. All of the children were facing the teacher, who was talking to them.

The teacher explained to the class that he was anxious to do more planning with them, but that the last time he had tried to do so the discussion had not gone well. He reminded them that too many people had talked at once and that other people, becoming bored, had begun doing independent work at their desks instead of listening to what was going on.

The children indicated in various ways that they remembered what had happened. They seemed to agree with the teacher that the discussion had not gone well, but they also indicated they wanted to try again.

The teacher asked them why they thought the discussion had not been successful. One child responded by saying that some children talked too long. Another said he could not hear some of the children when they were talking. The teacher went to the chalkboard and began to record the comments of the children: "Too long," "Children didn't speak loud enough," etc.

Soon one side of the board was filled with six items indicating what the children believed was unsatisfactory about their last discussion.

Another child raised his hand and accused a girl in the front of the room of talking too often during the last discussion. Two of her friends began defending her and a fuss developed. The teacher went over to them and asked if they thought this was the proper way to participate in a discussion. They agreed that it was not. Another child suggested that the teacher add "too much fussing" to the list on the chalkboard, because the same thing had happened during the last discussion.

After the teacher had added the seventh item to the list, he asked the children if they could think of anything else that had happened during the last discussion that they needed to add to their list. No one had any additions. He then read the list to them and asked them what they thought might be done so that future discussions would be more useful. No one seemed to have an immediate answer. Finally one child said, "Just don't do any of those things." The teacher accepted his answer seriously and asked him what might be done instead of each item on the board. "For example," said the teacher, "if some children talked too long before, then how should they behave in the future if we're going to have a good discussion?" One child responded by saying that they should take turns and that if a person talked too long, he was not giving someone else a chance to talk. The teacher nodded and went back to the chalkboard where he began another list which was called "Things To Do During Discussions." He listed "Take turns" and "Give others a chance to talk." He commented favorably on what the boy had said and asked the class how they might handle the next item on the list.

The teacher proceeded through the list of seven items, asking the children to put in their own words things they might do to carry on a better discussion. If a child had difficulty expressing his idea, the teacher tried to clarify it by repeating it in words that kept the thought but made the idea easier to add to the list.

When they had talked about each problem their list of "Things to Do During Discussions" read as follows:

Take turns.

Give others a chance to talk.

Wait until the person is finished talking.

Listen when someone else is talking.

Speak loud enough that all can hear.

Respect other people's ideas.

When the list was completed, the teacher asked them if they thought everything on the list of problems had been taken care of on the list of "Things to Do During Discussion." The children seemed pleased with the results of their efforts.

"Well, what do we do now?" asked the teacher. "We have our list of things to do. What do we do with it?"

One child suggested that they all copy the list and keep it in their notebooks, so they could use it during future discussions. Another child suggested that they make a chart and place it somewhere in the room as a reminder. The teacher asked the children what they thought of these two ideas. There was general agreement that both actions would be useful. The teacher suggested that they each copy the list and that his "Helper of the Week" begin thinking of an idea for the poster.

The teacher told the children that he was very pleased with the suggestions for good discussions that they had developed. He suggested that they have another discussion soon to make plans for their next social studies unit. He said he felt certain that their discussions would continue to get better now that they had talked about some of their problems and ways of solving them.

Analysis/Comment (Elementary)
In a discussion designed to help the students to improve their discussion skills, the elementary teacher revealed many competencies in using this strategy.

He made it clear at the beginning why he thought they needed to examine their problem in having discussions, and he helped them to reflect on their previous experience with the discussion method. He encouraged student participation and kept asking questions that revealed to them that their ideas were important to him. He was quite accepting of the thoughts the children shared and made supportive comments to let them know that he appreciated the contributions they were making to the discussion. He also kept the class moving toward a solution to the problem of how to have better discussions. Once they had agreed on some ways of handling future discussions, he encouraged them to use these ideas so that future discussions really would be more effective than those of the past.

The true test of the effectiveness of the use of the discussion strategy in this classroom will be in the planning session for the new social studies unit, as the students try to remember and use the standards that they developed cooperatively with the teacher.

CLASSROOM EXAMPLE (SECONDARY)
The following dialogue occurred at the beginning of a discussion conducted in a secondary school classroom by a nondirective teacher. (Note: In this and some of the other examples, numbers are used so that the analysis which follows can refer to specific sections of the example.)

1. TEACHER: For the past week we have been exploring the England of Elizabeth the First. Since it seems hard to discuss anything looking at the backs of people's heads, I have moved the desks into a circle. I think we agreed yesterday that we wanted to discuss the developments leading to England's emergence as a world power. Shall we begin?

2. SANDRA: (After a 15-second silence.) It feels sort of funny to sit in a circle.

3. (Teacher smiles.)

4. FRANK: The class looks different.

5. (Teacher smiles and nods agreement.)

6. HOWARD: I don't think I've seen some of these people face to face.

7. TEACHER: (After more silence.) I am thinking that I agree with Frank. The class does look a little dif-

ferent, but at least *I* usually see everyone's face. I'm wondering how others feel.
8. SUSAN: I like it.
9. MIKE: It's like Thanksgiving with everyone sitting around the table.
10. FRED: Boy, you must have a big family.
11. MIKE: Well, not quite this big.
12. HARRY: Maybe we ought to get a turkey.
13. JOE: Let's wait until we get to the Pilgrims.
14. (Class laughs and teacher joins in.)
15. MIKE: Yeah. We're supposed to be having a discussion.
16. HOWARD: All right, Mike, go ahead and discuss.
17. SUSAN: (To teacher.) How should we go about it, Mr. Harris?
18. TEACHER: Well, I guess there are a number of ways to begin, but I'm wondering if we are leaving Mike and Howard hanging.
19. MIKE: Oh, that's all right. Go ahead.
20. HOWARD: It's not all right with me. How come you cut me off, Susan?
21. SUSAN: I really hadn't thought about it. Sorry.
22. TEACHER: It's interesting to me the way groups make decisions. We were talking about how it felt to sit in a circle. Did we need to decide to leave that subject before going on?
23. FRED: It was Harry's turkey.
24. HARRY: And then Joe said wait for the Pilgrims.
25. JEANETTE: And here we are.
26. MARY: What do we do now?
27. JACK: I'd like to say something about this circle thing.
28. HARRY: Go ahead.
29. JACK: I think it makes it easier to talk.
30. HOWARD: I hope you don't stop.
31. JACK: Maybe I won't.
32. MARY: Should we talk about the topic?
33. MIKE: (Humorously.) We have to make a group decision.
34. (Class laughs.)
35. HOWARD: Let's agree that anybody can say what they're feeling even if it isn't on the topic.
36. MARY: But that would be confusing.
37. MIKE: What do you think, Mr. Harris?
38. TEACHER: I think it's an interesting idea, though Mary might be right. We need everyone's help in deciding.
39. MARY: You're not going to tell us the answer?
40. TEACHER: I'm not sure I know the answer, Mary. Perhaps we should know more about what Howard had in mind.
41. HARRY: What did you have in mind, Howie?
42. HOWARD: I just thought we could decide to leave the talk about sitting in a circle, which I'm getting tired of anyway, if we could feel free to return to it, like Jack did, if a thought hit us.
43. FRED: That sounds all right to me.
44. MARY: I still think it might get confusing, but if Mr. Harris doesn't know the answer, neither do I. I'd be willing to try it.
45. JEANETTE: Fine. Let's get on with it. Now, when the Spanish Armada sailed . . .
46. MIKE: Jeanette.
47. JEANETTE: Yes?
48. MIKE: Seriously, now. I don't want to cut you off, but I don't think the group really made this decision.
49. JEANETTE: Oh, for goodness sake!
50. JACK: I think he's right, Jeanette. If you start talking before you check the decision, how do you know that anyone's listening?
51. JEANETTE: Well, what do you want me to do?
52. SUSAN: What I should have done before. Ask everybody if they are ready to discuss the topic.

53. JEANETTE: Okay. (To class.) Are we ready to discuss the topic?
54. MIKE: (Breaking several seconds of silence.) I'm ready.
55. FRED: So am I.
56. (General murmur of assent with nodding heads.)
57. JEANETTE: All right. Now, I think we should start with the Armada. When Elizabeth began . . . [3]

Analysis/Comment (Secondary)
The teacher sets the scene (1), thus helping the class get started for an educational-diagnostic type discussion, as defined by Glasser, by referring to the common concern both students and teacher had identified "yesterday." From Sandra's early comment (2), it is apparent that the whole-class discussion in a circle format is something new for them. Fortunately, this teacher is willing to attempt "new" strategies to facilitate student learning. Certainly, the discussion strategy seems an appropriate choice for the history lesson planned.

Although the strategy is new to the pupils, the teacher has previously learned some of the "checkpoint" items. For instance, he accepts student comments while moving from nonverbal to verbal support of the students' rights to express feelings and opinions (4-7). In addition, he throws leadership back to the group (7)—in fact, allowing them to conduct the discussion while he assumes the role of a participant (16-18). Mike's remark (15) attempts to bring the conversation back to the original "education" emphasis for the class: England's emergence as a world power. But the teacher uses a probing question (18) to help students make personal value judgments about their own process behavior: *Are* they cutting off two of their fellow students? Here, Susan makes a value judgment on her own behavior (21).

The teacher continues, at this appropriate time, to focus pupil-thinking on the "circle" and the process of discussion in an open fashion (22). He seems to be following a predetermined plan of aiding students to diagnose what they do and might do in a discussion, as well as leading them into "subject-matter." A result of this dual emphasis is seen in Mike's comment (33) reflecting the growing idea that the students are responsible, to a reasonable extent, for their own learning and decision making. The subsequent interplay among Mike, Jeanette, and Jack (46-50) indicates that the students have taught themselves something about interacting with one another for group decision making. Perhaps this kind of outcome from discussion is at least equally important as the reasons for England's emergence as a world power. This discussion-oriented teacher evidently thinks so! Susan gives support to his belief when she confirms a personal learning (52) and implies that her future action in a group might be appropriately different.

Finally, a group decision is made (53-55), and Jeanette begins discussion of the topic (57). Note that the teacher has moved into the background again, yet it seems probable that the discussion will continue with direction and purpose, perhaps moreso as a result of the time spent with diagnosis and consideration of "process."

Overall, the checklist items constituted a major part of this teacher's use of the discussion strategy. He has evidenced many of those items offered on the competency worksheet and would probably build in others as needed. For instance, he could arrange students differently within the circle if the present arrangement becomes unsatisfactory; he could offer the chalkboard as a visual aid for listing reasons why England emerged as a world power when the discussion arrives at this point. He could reinforce the students' obligation to raise their hands to contribute—this being a management convenience for group maintenance if several students want to speak at once; and he could, easily enough, schedule with the students a follow-up discussion. In other words, he seems to be in control of a number of specific behaviors that comprise the discussion strategy.

NOTES
1. See William Glasser, *Schools Without Failure* (New York: Harper & Row, 1969); or Bruce Joyce and Marsha Weil, *Models of Teaching* (Englewood Cliffs, N.J.: Prentice-Hall, 1972), pp. 222-232.
2. J. J. Schwab and Evelyn Klinckmann, "Discussion in the Teaching of BSCS Biology," in Ronald T. Hyman (ed.), *Teaching, Vantage Points for Study* (New York: J. B. Lippincott Co., 1968), p. 459.
3. Alfred H. Gorman, *Teachers and Learners: The Interactive Process of Education* (Boston: Allyn and Bacon, 1969), pp. 95-98. (Reprinted with permission.)

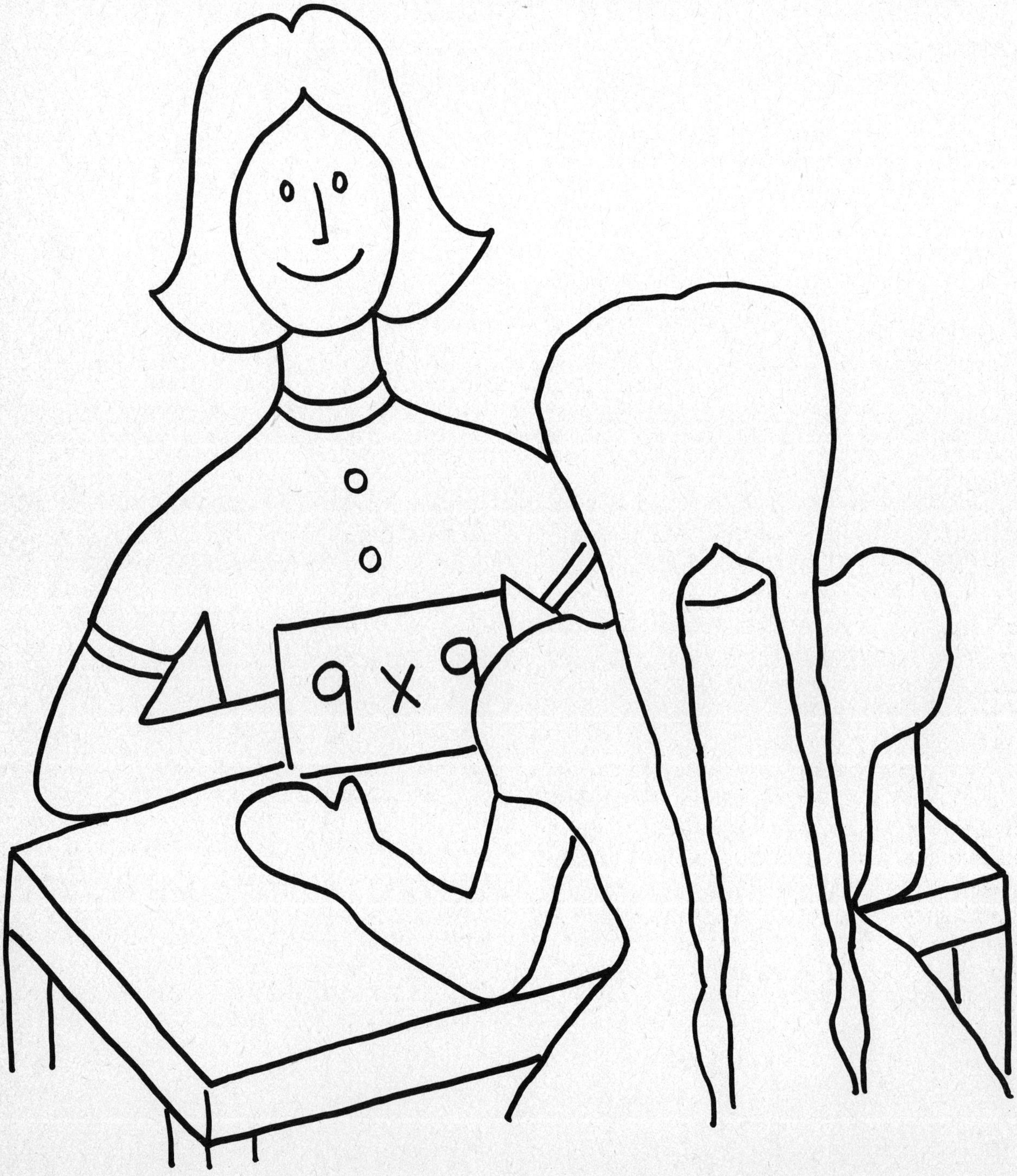
9 x 9

strategy 3

Drill and Practice

BACKGROUND

Teachers immemorial have emphasized the point that skills worth learning should be mastered accurately and completely; herein lies the role of drill and practice, which are really intended to bring about automatic accuracy and speed of performance in using the skills of any subject. Drill sometimes is distinguished from practice as a learning procedure, [1] drill being concerned with the fixation of specific associations for automatic recall and practice with improvement. Thus, one *drills* on spelling, but *practices* writing. We have included them as one strategy, because in classroom activities drill and practice are often used together.

Although drill and practice can be observed in most elementary and secondary classrooms today, the strategy is often used in an uncreative manner, which is probably influenced by its past usage in rote or passive learning situations that were common to the early American schools. The alert teacher, then, is looking for creative ways of using drill and practice to help pupils fix or refine basic motor skills, habits, and mental skills and to make them more meaningful, precise, and useful. Research reported on drill and practice, by the way, indicates that retention is facilitated when students learn skills in meaningful context.[2]

The positive approach to this "practice makes perfect" strategy, as stated by Hoover, revolves around two prior conditions: (1) that original learnings have been effective for the individual student; and (2) that learning is basically a problem-solving process, in that each learner (with the help of the teacher) explores various ways for making connections for himself, drilling and practicing until he has at least met the minimum standards for his objective.[3] Drill and practice—and this is the key to the strategy—are essentially individualized, even if in a group format in a regular classroom environment (see Classroom Examples).

In sum, the drill and practice strategy is largely an individualized problem-solving process, one based on development of initial learnings, varied contact, and repetition. Considered in this light, it need not be misused but rather may be seen by students and teachers for what it is—a helpful and viable part of regular classroom procedures and activities for learning.

COMPETENCY WORKSHEET FOR PLANNING AND OBSERVING

Checkpoints   **Observer Notes**

When using the drill and practice strategy, the teacher is usually observed performing the following behaviors:

_____ Checking to see if each student has some observable understanding of the material on which he will drill and practice.

_____ Considering individually, or with pupils in a group, the learning objective(s), e.g., are students aware of the purpose of the drill and practice? Is there sufficient motivation to begin? Do the students appreciate the need for these particular repetitive activities?

_____ Making available sufficient and appropriately selected drill and practice materials for each student, which will allow the student to reach successfully the objective(s) of the drill and practice session.

_____ Clarifying the plan for the progression of the session; e.g., this might include a "warm-up" or a demonstration before the start of the drill and practice, and a movement from relatively simple to more complex operations as the session proceeds.

_____ Providing conditions for the drill and practice that resemble as much as possible the "real-life" conditions in which the skill will be used.

_____ Establishing a time guideline; e.g., group drill and practice sessions often follow a 15- to 30-minute-per-session time guideline, depending on the teacher's judgment on where the "point of diminishing returns" is reached.

_____ Providing a variety of drill and practice situations until the objectives are achieved.

_____ Maintaining pupil motivation for continuing in drill and practice; e.g., involving students through their use of both touch and sound.

_____ Using positive verbal reinforcement.

_____ Using positive nonverbal reinforcement.

_____ Assessing student level of progress; e.g., walking around the classroom observing students and letting them know how well they are doing.

_____ Providing careful supervision, especially for pupils who are having trouble.

_____ Encouraging students who show sufficient competency in being able to get correct responses to proceed with drill and practice independent of the teacher, both inside and outside the classroom environment.

_____ Scheduling periodic reviews of skills learned in the drill and practice.

SOME ADVANTAGES

The following are often mentioned as some of the advantages of the drill and practice strategy:

- The method provides opportunities for "overlearning" specific skills, which tends to maximize retention.

- It may cause students to come to an increased appreciation of the skill they are learning through their drill and practice.

- The method focuses on specific components of learning tasks, so that students can concentrate on learning one skill at a time.

- The strategy aids development of a readily accessible and fixed repertoire of responses; e.g., certain difficult spelling words can be used without continually going to a dictionary.

- It may generate a feeling of success in pupils who are achieving mastery over a specific skill.

- The method enables individual students to find a skill applicable, extendable, or transferable to related learning situations or problems; e.g., drill and practice in using the telephone in elementary school may aid the child in answering and using the phone at home.

- The multiple varieties of the strategy can relieve any boredom that might accompany its use and, at the same time, can enhance the development of skills. (See Classroom Examples.)

- The strategy can enable both the students and the teacher to recognize quite clearly the need for further work on the skill being developed.

- It offers an easy method for students to use in improving their own skill learning.

- Drill is a familiar technique to most parents and is accepted in many communities as a valid instructional strategy.

SOME DISADVANTAGES

The following are often mentioned as some of the disadvantages of the drill and practice strategy:

- Classroom drill and practice experiences without careful supervision may permit students to practice an incorrect or inappropriate response.

- The strategy may cause the teacher or the students to assume that mere repetition of a skill is sufficient for mastery.

- Drill and practice can be boring and monotonous if students do not see any meaning or future use of the skills being learned.

- The method is inappropriate for direct development of concepts and values.

- It requires careful preparation, with consideration given to the needs of individual students. Some teachers may not prepare sufficiently, assuming the drill and practice method can take care of itself once it is introduced and started.

- The strategy may be viewed as an interpretation of learning that overemphasizes the acquisition of facts.

- The individualized nature of drill, when applied in a group setting, makes it extremely difficult for the teacher to determine whether a given student is ready for a change in pace or contents in the drill and practice exercises.

CLASSROOM EXAMPLE (ELEMENTARY)

The teacher in this self-contained second-grade classroom is working with a small reading group at the front of the room, while the other children in the class are involved in practice exercises planned to assist them in the development of their reading skills. The materials being used by the children have been selected on the basis of their reading level. The children at their desks are moving through these materials on their own. The teacher has asked them first to complete their assignments in the practice books and then to select another activity on which they would like to work.

Several children have completed their reading practice activities and are busy at their desks reading books from the library that they had selected the day before. Another child has pulled out a set of homemade flashcards which represent number facts that he did not know the last time he was given an arithmetic test. He is calling out the answers quietly to himself and then checking on the back of the card to see if his answers are correct.

Another child has asked a friend to go back to the science corner of the room to help her feed the fish. The two of them are responsible this week for taking care of the aquarium and they know that they must feed the fish regularly. Two other children are in the science corner, using the new microscope that the teacher recently taught them how to operate.

Another girl appears to be drilling herself on spelling words for the weekly test. She has the

DRILL AND PRACTICE

spelling list before her and is trying to spell each word aloud and then write it down on paper. A friend comes by and asks if she needs any help, and the girl accepts the offer. The friend pulls up a chair by the girl and calls out the words to her.

By this time, the teacher has completed her work with the reading group and is moving about the room checking on the progress of the pupils, as she reminds the next group that it is time to come to the front of the class where she will be working with them.

The children whose group just met return to their desks to begin their practice work, followed by independent activities.

Analysis/Comment (Elementary)
Formal, large group drill is most uncommon in modern elementary schools. Usually students are taught a skill and then given many opportunities to use it in a variety of situations.

This elementary classroom was a good example. The students using the reading practice materials had been given their assignments following their group session. The teacher thus had a fairly good idea of the children's ability to complete their assignments before these were given to them. If the children had needed additional help, they could have either asked the teacher when she moved about the room checking on their progress or they could have asked another child.

The other children were free to select additional independent activities which were quite varied. As you recall, the children were observed to be:

- practicing their reading skills through independent, recreational reading
- drilling on a set of homemade flashcards
- practicing the appropriate care of pets
- practicing the effective use of the microscope
- drilling on spelling words

If observation of the classroom had lasted for a longer period of time, many more examples of drill and practice would undoubtedly have been seen. All of the activities observed were designed to help the students to master through drill and practice the skills under study.

CLASSROOM EXAMPLE (SECONDARY)
The following lesson illustrating the drill strategy at work is applicable to the development of mental skills in general, whether they be in the area of foreign language, English, music, social studies, science, or any other discipline in a school's curriculum.

On entering their Spanish class, the eighth-grade students were greeted with a chalkboard notice: "*As You Enter* — Study Vocab. in Chp. #5." The teacher stood by the door directing students to their assigned seats until all had entered. He then moved throughout the class answering individual's questions and helping—firmly, at times—pupils at least to look at, if not study, the vocabulary lesson assigned in Chapter 5 of the textbook supplement. After about 7 to 10 minutes had passed, he spoke to the class in Spanish: "Please close your books and look up here." Then, back to English: "All of you are at the point where knowledge of some additional vocabulary would help you. If you think back on what we were doing yesterday and the week before, you can probably tell me why I'd say this. Who has a suggestion?"

Response from students seemed to clarify the idea that they had been weak in responding, in Spanish, to questions asked on the chapters on which they had been working in their modern foreign language textbook. Moreover, several students noted that they had "drawn blanks" rather frequently in trying to converse in Spanish with one another during recent class conversations led by the teacher.

At this juncture the teacher asked, "Do you think it's worthwhile to increase your vocabularies in Spanish? Why?" He allowed students to discuss for a while and to air their views and feelings.

"Most of you seem 'positive' toward learning vocabulary," continued the teacher, "so today we are going to do a little systematic, creative drill on words that begin with g, as offered in Chapter 5. I've selected these because a lot of the words you've just been looking over can be used in our class conversations and in our regular work, and you've already been exposed to some of them. For instance, what is *gato*? Raise your hand if you know." (All but five students raised their hands.) "Keep your hands up if you are correct; it means . . . what?" A student responds, "Cat." The teacher affirmed. All hands stayed up. The teacher did a few more of these "warm-up" checks, giving verbal praise and nodding and smiling as students responded. From his observation, it seemed as if the same five students were generally not raising their hands or were dropping them, indicating an incorrect translation. But most of the students were doing pretty well, even if they were hesitant on certain words.

"OK," said the teacher, "now let's be more sure that each of you is learning as many of the vocabulary words in Chapter 5 as you can. Remember, you need to kind of 'over-learn' them, so they can be *used* by you, not just so you can recall them a few minutes after you've memorized them. I've got some learning stations around the classroom that will help you. They all stress the same *g* words. Let me go over the general directions with you. Then you can go to the stations. Reassemble as a 'class of the whole' in about 30 minutes for a 'wrap-up' drill. Here are the directions:

> First, visit as many stations as you like; start wherever you choose and stay as long as you find the work helpful and meaningful and challenging.
>
> Second, follow the specific directions at each station. Competency progress checks are included, and I'll be giving you feedback on how you are doing.
>
> Third, work at your own speed but, all things being equal, try to 'do' at least two stations.
>
> Fourth, let me give you an overview: *Station 1* is recommended especially for 'beginners.' If you aren't too sure about the vocabulary in Chapter 5, start here. At this station you will work in pairs, using flashcards for learning the vocabulary words and saying them as they appear in sentences. *Station 2* is recommended especially for those with 'medium' competency on the Chapter 5 vocabulary. Here you will be working in helping trios with the tape recorders. You will hear me ask a question, and one trio member will need to respond—using the Chapter 5 vocabulary—while the second member listens

and critiques, and the third checks the correct answer for aiding the critique. Then of course, switch roles. *Station 3* is recommended especially for those who feel they have a sound grasp of all or almost all of the vocabulary in Chapter 5. Here you will be writing original stories—creative or news—using the words of Chapter 5. These will be forwarded to our school newspaper for publication and will be posted for the upcoming P.T.A. 'Back-to-School' night.

"I'll be around to help anyone who needs help," the teacher concluded. "Just let me know!"

During the classwork, the teacher paid special attention to the five or so students who seemed most unable to cope during the warm-ups. He directed them to Station 1, for example, and moved around the class observing the efforts and progress of all the students—helping where appropriate. Finally, when students reassembled at the conclusion of the class, the teacher talked over the drill experience with them and stated that he would give each student a progress report after he had had a chance to look at the objective checks turned in at the respective stations. He promised, "We'll have a check-up on these words soon, in the sense that you'll need them for our basic text work coming up; in addition, you can be better prepared for our faculty invitation party next month, where you'll need to talk in Spanish. Also, tomorrow we'll schedule a review of the Chapter 5 words. So keep practicing. Try today's words at home, for instance! Let's spend the last few minutes today, however, in another kind of drill. We'll play the 'baseball' game. Boys will be one team; girls, the other. If you can answer my question based on the same Chapter 5 words, you score a hit. If you miss, it's an 'out.' Three outs and the other team comes up. The bigger score at the end of the period wins."

In a short while, the period ended and the class was dismissed.

Analysis/Comment (Secondary)

In this example, it may be noted that the checkpoint items are being followed in the same general order in which they appear on the competency worksheet. Perhaps the teacher has been using a similar checklist to train himself on the drill strategy! At any rate, he uses the strategy rather effectively.

The "warm-up" checks and, of course, the "As You Enter" activity provide students a chance to become familiar with the material on which they will drill. The teacher, in addition, has clarified with the students the purpose of the day's work. Although the teacher does state the amount of material to be dealt with (all the g vocabulary in Chapter 5), the objective is not mentioned in precise terms. One of the things the teacher might do in reteaching through drill would be to nail down with the students the precise objective or objectives of the lesson, perhaps in behavioral terms.

From evidence in the example, the material is both available and appropriate for drill; that is, vocabulary building is clearly in the mental skill area and can be built on and "polished." Presumably, each student has the text. The teacher, in addition, has set a progression for the class: from a diagnostic "warm-up" to a series of three increasingly complex learning stations to a kind of pressurized, speed drill—the baseball game. All of these, with their emphasis on oral and written use of vocabulary in context and in interaction, really provide what is listed on the competency worksheet as "practice conditions resembling the conditions in which the skill will be used." To be sure, vocabulary is related intimately in real life to contextual and human considerations.

Although drill is the name of the game throughout the period, the variety of drill experiences in both small and large group situations—warm-up, station exercises, game, with no one of these parts exceeding 30 minutes—should maintain a high level of learner involvement. Throughout these activities, the teacher allows students to work at their own paces, but he has also planned that they should finish the "warm-up," two of three centers, and a game prior to the end of class. This suggests the overall pace *he* expects is a rather rapid one—whether he admits it or not. It is difficult to infer from the example just what the teacher finds during his supervision. If, however, he has at least five slower students, with others perhaps not maintaining and learning at a rapid pace, it might be a worthy idea to continue the baseball game or hold it in a review period. Perhaps even the stations should be run again at a later date. In sum, the lesson seems a lot for one class period, at least in terms of the slower students getting maximum benefit from all the drill activities. Consistent supervision and spot checks of student work can help the teacher decide for himself if the lesson plan needs to be modified as the class goes on.

Other teacher behaviors are interesting and in line with the strategy checkpoints. He encourages pupils to practice outside of class—at home, in this case—and he schedules a review for the next session, thus putting students in a position to reinforce for themselves their initial learnings. Further, it is helpful to recognize in the example that the teacher's behavior has included giving positive verbal and nonverbal reinforcement (saying "good" and smiling), allowing students to direct and assess their own learning (as with the helping trio at Station 2), and providing for individual differences (by directing the five slower students to Station 1). Finally, the teacher aids the students in seeing how what they are learning ties in to a larger context, that of the classroom world and the "real" world as represented by the upcoming party where students will need to speak Spanish. Both in these coming events and in what went before, the teacher has successfully made use of drill in itself and—as is quite usual with drill and practice—in combination with other instructional procedures (such as learning stations), to help his students help themselves.

NOTES

1. Harry N. Rivlin (ed.), *Encyclopedia of Modern Education* (Port Washington, New York: Kennikat Press, 1969), Vol. 1.

2. Chester W. Harris (ed.), *Encyclopedia of Educational Research* (New York: Macmillan Co., 1960), p. 857.

3. Kenneth H. Hoover (ed.), "Review and Drill: Valuable but Widely Misused Teaching Techniques," in James A. Johnson and Roger C. Anderson, *Secondary Student Teaching Readings* (Glenview, Ill.: Scott, Foresman and Co., 1971), p. 130.

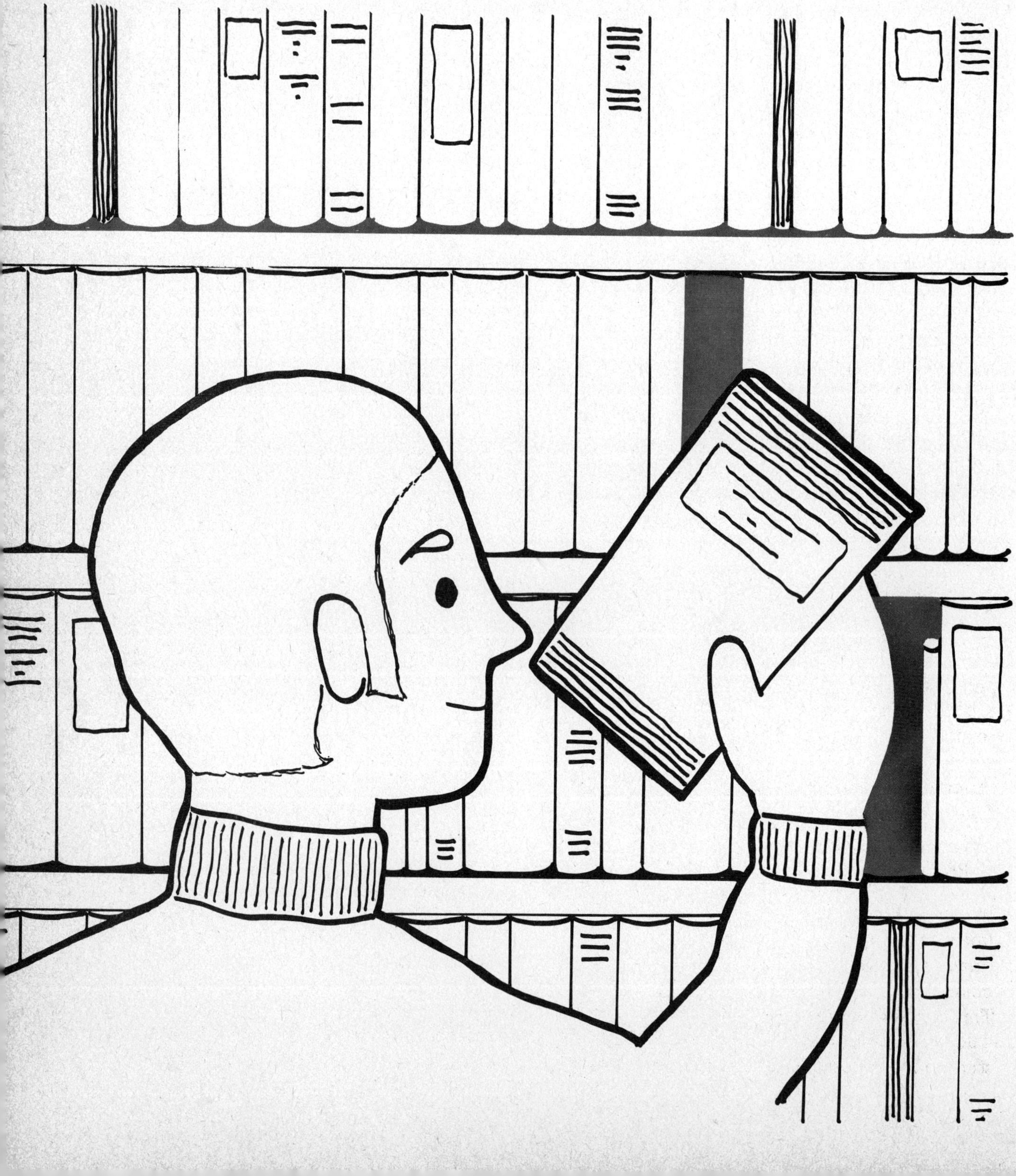

strategy 4

Independent Study

BACKGROUND

Although the use of independent study as a teaching strategy for helping students move toward and reach educational objectives is not new, there was a renewed interest in using this strategy in both elementary and secondary schools during the 1960s. Evidence of this is that in the mid-1950s *The Education Index*, a listing of writings in the field, contained only a few articles on the topic, while by the mid-1960s forty to fifty articles were being listed annually.[1]

Much of the renewed interest in this strategy for passing the knowledge of one generation on to the next has been attributed to the national concern for providing academically challenging programs for the exceptional student in our society. This concern, which had begun at the university level after World War I, was intensified when Russia's *Sputnik*, the first satellite to orbit the earth, was successfully launched in 1957. Today, however, many educators would agree that independent study should be available for all pupils—not just the academically gifted.[2]

Although independent study is interpreted in many different ways, it is defined in the *Dictionary of Education* as "educational activity carried on by an individual seeking self-improvement, usually but not always self-initiated." This broad definition could include anything the students do independently, from supervised study in a classroom to flying to Mexico during the spring vacation for a study of the Aztec Indians.

For the purpose of this discussion, we will focus on the type of planned study done by an individual under the guidance of a teacher-counselor, which involves the identification of a problem, topic, or project and moves the student though a process concluding with an evaluative activity that pulls together the learnings gained from the study. This method of study may be organized in formal steps, as suggested in the Analysis/Comment for the elementary Classroom Example, or in an informal manner, as illustrated by the secondary example.

As both of these classroom examples indicate, the type of independent study under discussion can take place in any school setting and does not require special equipment or personnel. Alternatively, it can be the major means of learning in a comprehensive program where the facilities are designed and the personnel are selected and trained to work with students in independent study programs. For some students, independent study may be limited to the acquistion of understandings through seeking the answers to problems posed by teachers. Or it may involve self-directed learning that is separate from course requirements.

Our more precise definition of independent study can take place at the elementary level as well as the secondary. Although there are individual differences among both small children and older children in their success with independent study, there is evidence that pupils of all ages and of a wide range of abilities can achieve as well as and in many cases better than can students in classrooms in which this instructional strategy is not used. Research has also revealed a great variety of means for implementing independent study which range from providing elaborate, technically equipped carrels to rearranging classroom furniture.[3]

In 1964, John Gardner wrote in his book *Self-Renewal: The Individual and the Innovative Society* that the ultimate goal of education should be "to shift to the individual the burden of pursuing his own education." Independent study in all of its various assorted forms can contribute to the achievement of that goal.[4]

COMPETENCY WORKSHEET FOR PLANNING AND OBSERVING

Checkpoints

Observer Notes

When using the independent study strategy, the teacher is usually observed performing the following behaviors:

_____ Identifying through interviews, inventories, and tests the individual interests and abilities of the students that might be used in planning independent study activities.

_____ Locating materials and experiences that correspond to the needs of the pupils' interests and abilities.

_____ Planning with each student how he will proceed with the independent study activities; e.g., a contract arrangement might be agreed on.

_____ Helping students to assess their independent study skills; e.g., note-taking, outlining, using bibliographies, using resources other than printed ones, preparing reports both oral and written.

_____ Allowing an appropriate amount of time for the student to engage in the independent study.

_____ Providing help and encouragement as indicated by student need.

INDEPENDENT STUDY

_____ Helping the students to evaluate their progress toward the agreed-on objectives of the study; e.g., reviewing logs kept by the students that provide a record of their activities.

_____ Conducting group discussions of those involved in independent study, for the purpose of sharing their experiences and learnings during the study as well as at its completion.

_____ Evaluating with the students the final results of their studies.

_____ Assessing with the student what he has learned from the study that might assist him in selecting and conducting future independent studies; e.g., use of new resources, development of new study skills.

SOME ADVANTAGES

The following are often mentioned as advantages of the independent study strategy:

- It allows the student to pursue his topic with as much depth as he wishes and to be as creative as his talents permit; e.g., a secondary student might investigate the adolescent dimensions of a psychology course and produce an 8-mm. film to report his findings.

- It may be carried out in any school, regardless of the organization of the staff.

- The strategy does not normally require additional equipment.

- It is appropriate for all areas of the curriculum.

- It enhances a student's motivation, because he is often involved in selecting what he plans to study.

- It helps bridge the gap between the school and the community because it can occur in a variety of settings. Older students are encouraged to go out and use community resources in their independent studies. Members of the community with special talents may also serve as resource people by coming to the school to help students who are exploring topics related to their areas of specialization.

- The method allows students to pursue individual interests within the required curriculum as well as to supplement the curriculum.

- It emphasizes the learner's responsibility and accountability. The student must learn to use the skills of inquiry as he identifies his topic of study, makes plans, gathers data, summarizes what he has found, and draws conclusions from his findings. This promotes a feeling of independence and self-discipline.

- It allows students to develop knowlege and skills that cannot be obtained as well in a regular classroom setting; e.g., an elementary student interested in studying how newspapers are written and produced could only read and use multi-media materials in the regular classroom. Through independent study, however, he could arrange to visit a newspaper office and learn about newspaper production firsthand.

- The strategy contributes to personal involvement on the part of the learner. A student doing an independent study cannot sit passively in a classroom, allowing others to take the initiative in raising questions and participating in discussions.

SOME DISADVANTAGES
The following are often mentioned as disadvantages of the individual study strategy:

- There is little social interaction, unless planned for.

- The strategy is difficult for students to handle effectively, if they have been used to conforming and competing in group settings only.

- It is viewed to be ineffective by many teachers, parents, and administrators, who believe that group activities provide the best setting for learning.

- It arouses the concern of some parents and students over whether or not students are learning what they should for promotion to the next grade or for college entrance requirements.

- It requires a low teacher-pupil ratio for adequate planning, counseling, and supervision. Teachers need to be available on a regular basis for conferring with students.

- It can be expensive when used on a comprehensive basis in a school, because the strategy may require adjustments in the use of space, personnel, and materials. Some educators believe that a comprehensive program for independent study requires five types of facilities: study and work centers for each subject field, a library, a conference area, relaxation space, and an "intensive care" area for those students who are not yet able to assume responsibility for their own learning.

- The strategy requires additional adult supervision, which may be difficult to arrange. Adult assistance may be needed at school, on the way to sites where the study is taking place, and at the place of study.

- The method can be uncomfortable for some teachers, because it requires a different type of relationship between a student and teacher. The teacher is placed in a position of helping the student to become more independent in his learning activities, rather than being the major souce of the student's knowledge. Even a teacher who believes strongly in independent study may find it difficult to adjust to this working relationship, particularly at the secondary level, where the maturity of the student allows greater freedom to go outside the school.

- The strategy could have an undesirable effect on a student's thinking and attitude. A secondary student could become so intensely involved in attaining the goals of his independent study that he forgets how it fits into the overall program, or a student who already feels alienated from the school might find his independent study so interesting that he quits school and pursues this new interest, which excites him more.

CLASSROOM EXAMPLE (ELEMENTARY)
In this middle-elementary classroom, the children had just completed a unit on their state, which involved them in group investigation activities. For purposes of variety, the teacher has suggested that they each select any topic of interest that they would like to investigate on their own for the next week or two. The teacher discussed this with the class and most of the children were immediately able to think of something they wanted to learn more about. She told them to talk with their mothers and dads about it, as well, in case their studies required any help from

adults, and to bring in the next day answers to six questions that she placed on the chalkboard.

On the following day, most of the children brought in their answers, and the teacher planned time for them to talk with her about what they would like to work on independently. She arranged for all of the children to be engaged in a recreational reading activity that did not require her immediate assistance, while she has conferences with those who have decided on the topics for their independent studies.

As each child comes to her desk, he brings a piece of paper that has his answers to the following questions:

What would you like to do for your study?

Why would you like to do this?

What kind of help (people, materials) will you need?

How long do you think it will take?

Have you talked this over with your mother or dad?

How do you think this study will help you?

The teacher reviews each response with the child and makes appropriate comments. If the project appears to be too difficult or time consuming, she tries to help the child look at his idea a bit more realistically. If he seems unwilling to make a change, she allows the student to continue, hoping that he will learn through his own experiences how much he can accomplish toward completing the study that he has selected. She gives each student advice concerning the resources that are available for study within the classroom and the library. She also suggests that each student keep a daily work record, as a way of helping him to evaluate his progress and as an easy way for her to see what he has done.

Following the conferences, she explains to the remaining members of the class that she will make similar arrangements for them to talk with her on the next day and that she hopes everyone will have decided on a topic by the end of the week. She compliments the children with whom she has talked today on the interesting topics they have selected, and she asks all of the class if they would like to share their individual projects with the class when they are finished. Some of the children look enthusiastic about doing so, while others shake their heads, indicating they do not think it is such a good idea. The teacher suggests they talk about sharing the projects at a later time.

She reminds the children that today is library day and that it is almost time for them to leave their regular classroom. She suggests that the children who have already conferred with her begin to look for materials that might assist them in their studies. She also suggests that those who have not decided on a topic might possibly think of an idea as they look through some of the materials in the library. She indicates that both she and the librarian will be glad to help them.

Analysis/Comment (Elementary)
There are several ways in which independent study can take place in an elementary setting. These activities can be individual assignments that students assume responsibility for as a part of the regular curriculum, or they can be topics of interest that complement and supplement the required course of study. In this particular classroom example, the teacher has completed a unit of study that was a part of the basic curriculum. Independent study activities could have been planned as a part of this unit. Instead, the teacher used the group investigation strategy to help the children reach the objectives of the unit of work.

The teacher obviously has enough flexibility with her social studies curriculum to plan independent studies selected by the children on the basis of their interests. She assumes that the children will select topics that truly interest them and that through personal conferences she will be able to help them develop realistic plans for their independent work. She also asks each child to discuss this project with his mother or dad, so that they will know what the child is studying and, hopefully, will offer their help and support as needed.

The list of six questions for the children to think through before talking with her helped her, in several ways, to perform the behaviors usually associated with the independent study strategy. Because the children had already thought about these questions before the conference and in some cases might have discussed them with one or both of their parents, the teacher was able to offer assistance in the conference. She was able to help match the child with available resources, to review his own personal resources for accomplishing his goals, and to set a realistic time frame for his activities. She was able to learn how motivated he actually was to complete the study. She also helped each individual to clarify his objectives and to be able to state them in terms related to his own behavior. This was the purpose of the question: "How do you think this study will help you?"

Another step taken at the conference was to get the child started on a procedure for keeping a record of his progress for his own self-evaluation and for evaluation by the teacher. The teacher suggested a daily log that would include a brief entry telling what had been accomplished each day. If he had not accomplished much, then the mere writing in his log might serve as an incentive to do more on the next day. Certainly, the logs would be helpful to the teacher in talking with each child about the progress being made in the study.

The teacher does not mention anything, in this observed lesson, about conducting group sessions during which the children can discuss their progress with one another and perhaps share some of the things they are learning in the process of completing the study. Perhaps she suggested this in her opening comments to them on the previous day. She does, during this example, indicate the possibility that the students might share some of the projects when they have completed them, but the reaction to this idea is mixed, so she lets it drop for the moment.

Another thing that is unclear from this example is how much the children already know about independent study. She does ask them to think about the kind of help they may need, but the example does not reveal how the teacher has introduced the steps of independent inquiry that would include the following stages, as defined by Rooze and Foerster:[5]

identifying the problem

identifying sources of data

gathering data

evaluating data

drawing conclusions

evaluating conclusions

communicating ideas

She has helped them to move through the first two phases and has encouraged them to begin using the library during the next class period. She also indicates that she and the librarian will be there to help them. Perhaps she has already taught them the steps mentioned above, but the classroom did not reveal any chart that would indicate this was true, nor did she refer to these steps during the example. Because this was a group of middle-elementary children, it seems most important that they become more aware of the steps involved in the independent study process and of the skills needed to pursue this process successfully. There is no evidence in the example that this has been done.

There is evidence, however, to indicate that the children are off to a good start under the guidance of their teacher and that their independent pursuit of personal objectives will probably be a most enriching experience for all of them.

CLASSROOM EXAMPLE (SECONDARY)

The career education class considered in this secondary example normally requires that students work independently, that is, that they pursue their own courses of action for the investigation, experimentation, and application of concepts, problems, or skills of their choice. The course is an elective one in the industrial arts curriculum. Students wishing to take it are screened to see if they demonstrate strong commitment for the responsibility and the freedom they will exercise during their independent study activities. Tests to indicate student skill levels are also given as a part of the screening. Each student accepted into the class is helped to enter a work experience program related to his interest, so that he will develop salable skills or gain appropriate career information.

The way the program works is simple. After the student is accepted into the program, the teacher helps him find a job or project. Most of the students have a "leg up" on this before entering the program. Both the guidance counselor and the teacher are available for those needing additional help. Then the student works out his "contract" with the teacher. This is a way for both to know what the student is about and to set some goals, deadlines, and minimum acceptable standards. Next, the student engages in his work in the community or in school, checking with the teacher as agreed in the contract. Occasionally, all of the students meet for group discussion. Each student also has several counseling sessions with the teacher, who makes it a point to check with any employers of his students. At the end of the course, each student is given credit toward graduation if he fulfills the contract.

One very interesting observation is that college-bound students are in the course along with vocational and trade-oriented students. One young man, for example, is involved with the local church in setting up its day-care center. He is considering entering a four-year college program in early childhood education after his June graduation. This elective course incorporating the independent study strategy offers him a fine opportunity to see for himself if this is the career for him.

Another student works strictly in the industrial arts shop, where she has selected from a variety of activity areas—for example, wood, plastics, power equipment, graphics—and is now designing a project she wishes to make. She is the manager of her own activities, including maintaining records of attendance, recording materials purchased, and reporting the usage of power equipment. She also determines the procedural steps of her work. In respect to these, she will go to self-instructional materials for learning how to use an oxyacetylene torch. When ready, she will ask the teacher to check her out on the torch. Upon receiving an "OK" rating and finally finishing her project, she will presumably complete the necessary paper work and thereby fulfill her contract with the teacher. Her original interest in being "something like a welder" is becoming more keen than ever—fostered by the experience and pride of accomplishment she is gaining. No letter grade will be given unless requested, by the way, but the paper work will include a competency report that she and the teacher will mark in accord with their agreement on her observable skills. She will also be reminded by the teacher of where she can find information available on post-high-school technical programs in the area—at community colleges, for instance.

The classmates of the two students mentioned are engaged with similar experiences, as this brief look at the independent study strategy in operation ends. It seems to be working for the benefit of both teacher and students.

Analysis/Comment (Secondary)

In this example, the independent study strategy is functioning effectively to foster student learning. The industrial arts teacher has done the job—through screening—of testing and checking individual interests and abilities for coping with independent study procedures. The students themselves, with teacher guidance, have selected their own independent study emphasis. Moreover, they are "tied in" to a helping relationship with the teacher through the contract agreed upon. The built-in checks and group discussions can also help the individual students assess and improve their skills and proceed with the independent study activities, which they have pretty much set for themselves as they become increasingly capable of so doing.

The major teacher characteristics of supervising and helping that are necessary for this strategy to enable student learning are being followed. The girl, for instance, has materials available that can teach her how to use the torch, and the teacher insists that she be competent in performing with it before she can use it on her own. He also confers with the young man's employer and, presumably observes the boy at work in the off-campus setting. Although we might note a lack of formal encouragement in the example, the overall teacher approach certainly lends itself to a happy, if business-like, atmosphere. In addition, in line with the checklist, we note that a time commitment is built into the contract. Further, the contract should, and likely does, have some specific and agreed-on ways in which student progress can be evaluated. The teacher's greater interest should be in gauging the individual's increasing ability to learn, rather than in judging the project. But both can be evaluated. In the boy's case, as with the girl and most students involved with independent study, evaluation of progress is a personal thing. The teacher can provide the tools, the situation, some criteria, the help, even additional interpretation. But whether one goes into teaching and the other becomes a welder is a decision the students themselves can make, as they consider their own growth and where it might lead them. The independent study provides teachers with a vehicle for aiding students in this endeavor.

NOTES

1. Charles A. Wedemeyer, "Independent Study: Overview," *Encyclopedia of Education* (New York: Macmillan Co., and Free Press, 1971), p. 548.

2. J. Lloyd Trump, "Independent Study: The Schools," *Encyclopedia of Education* (New York: Macmillan Co., and Free Press, 1971), p. 561

3. *Ibid.*

4. John Gardner, *Self-Renewal: The Individual and the Innovative Society* (New York: Harper, 1964), p. 12.

5. Gene E. Rooze and Leona M. Foerster, *Teaching Elementary School Social Studies: A New Perspective* (Columbus, Ohio: Charles E. Merrill, 1972), p. 72.

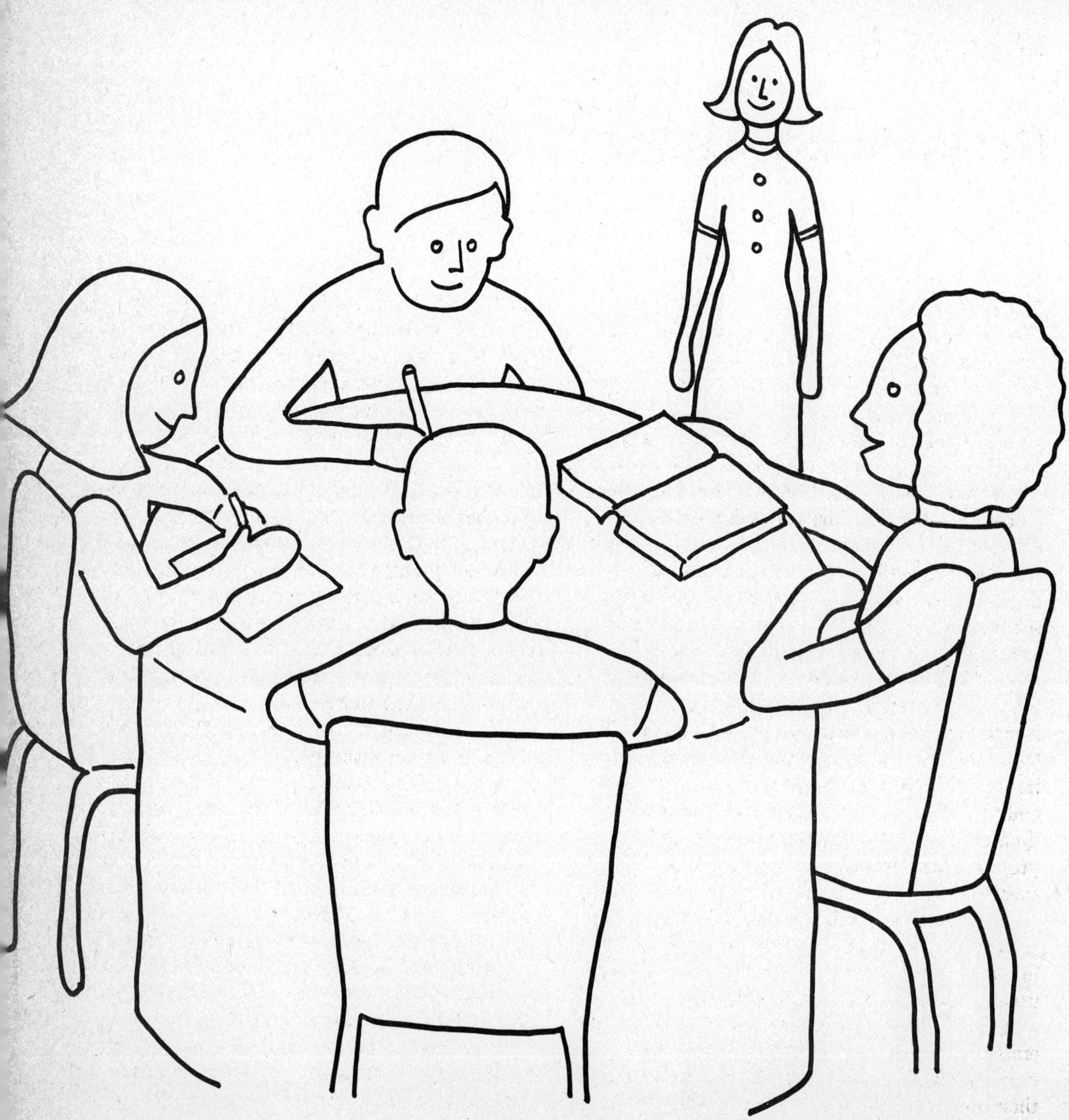

strategy 5

Group Investigation

BACKGROUND

Group investigation has been a natural process for human beings since prehistoric times. In *Men in Groups*, the author explores the necessity for early humans to work together for survival and emphasizes how this need continues today in our age of increased interdependence.[1]

It was not until this century, however, that educators began to realize the full potential of group investigation as a legitimate strategy in the teaching-learning process. John Dewey, the psychologist and philosopher who believed that school was not preparation for life but life itself, initiated a school at the University of Chicago in 1902 to try out some of his revolutionary theories. Dewey was director of the School of Education at the university and organizer of the laboratory school for two years. Because he believed that individuals learned in a social context and that there should be opportunities for children to work together in groups to investigate problems and interests, Dewey encouraged his staff to use group investigation activities.[2]

Group investigation as defined today is the activity of a group of students, ordinarily small in number, organized for a study. The group is usually made up of students who select, or are placed together by their teachers, to work cooperatively toward answers and solutions to common concerns or problems. The students clarify their objectives, plan procedures, gather information, analyze their findings, draw conclusions, and often report their findings back to the total class. The focus of the group investigation can be related to a larger topic under study by the total class or to a topic of interest only to a small group conducting the investigation.

It seems important at this point to emphasize the fact that this section on group investigation does not examine small group *instruction*, a practice that is common to elementary schools. Many elementary teachers group their children for instruction in reading and arithmetic as well as other curriculum areas, for the purpose of individualizing instruction. In the small group, however, teachers may use a variety of strategies for teaching the children. The small group is merely an organizational device for the purpose of having a more manageable group of learners. Small group instruction is often practiced in secondary classrooms as well. The strategy that we refer to as group *investigation*, however, requires an observable pattern of behavior on the part of the teacher, in order to help the students accomplish the objectives of their work together and to improve their ability to work within a group.

Although the skills developed through group investigation have value both for the class as a whole as well as for the individuals in the class, many authorities believe that the most legitimate use of group investigation is when this method appears to be better than individual study for reaching goals identified by the students.

"The basic rationale for developing skill in group work," according to Kenneth Rehage, "derives from the idea that the successful achievement of many purposes, both in school and outside school, demands cooperative action of several individuals. Cooperative action that is successful in turn depends upon a variety of skills on the part of participating individuals. Such skills, like other skills, are learned through practice. The school is a particularly appropriate place to get the needed practice. Some of the school subjects like the social studies can provide situations which are particularly well suited for practice in the application of group work skills."[3]

Group investigation is probably more commonly used at the elementary level, especially the middle and intermediate levels. Many secondary teachers, however, particularly in junior high schools, have found this approach a most effective way of teaching, especially in the areas of social studies, English, and science.

Very little research has been done in reference to the use of group investigation as a method within a classroom setting. Theoretical guidelines have been suggested for the size of the group, for time to be spent in the investigation, and for the composition of the group, however. These guidelines suggest that the groups should be small (5 to 6 students), should be given sufficient time to adequately accomplish the stated objectives, and should be be organized on the basis of choice.[4]

All varieties of group investigation, however, have one common characteristic: Students plan their own learning through open-ended tasks rather than just carrying out the teacher's assignment for them.[5]

COMPETENCY WORKSHEET FOR PLANNING AND OBSERVING

Checkpoints   **Observer Notes**

When using the group investigation strategy, the teacher is usually observed performing the following behaviors:

_____ Assessing how much group investigation the students have done during previous school work.

_____ Determining what possibilities for group investigation are available within the curriculum.

_____ Identifying the skills needed by the group in accomplishing its investigation.

_____ Reviewing the basic procedures for group investigation with the students.

_____ Helping children identify the topics or problems to be explored.

_____ Providing guidance to children as they organize into groups and select leaders.

_____ Serving as a resource to the groups as they make initial plans and survey available resources.

_____ Judging whether or not the plans made by the students are within their range of abilities.

_____ Supervising carefully the students' activities, so that assistance is available when needed.

_____ Hiding frustrations when poor student leadership is selected.

_____ Helping children recognize the qualities of leadership needed for effective group investigation.

_____ Closing out activities tactfully if progress is not proceeding in a positive direction.

_____ Assisting the students in analyzing and drawing conclusions from their findings.

_____ Assisting the students in selecting an appropriate manner for presenting their findings to others.

_____ Assisting the group in evaluating the effectiveness of their efforts.

SOME ADVANTAGES
The following are often mentioned as advantages of the group investigation strategy:

- It allows students to use inquiry skills that many educators believe will better prepare learners for the future than will more traditional teaching-learning strategies.

- It provides opportunities for more intensive investigation of a study or problem.

- The strategy is conducive to developing student leadership and teaching the skills of discussion and group processes.

- It enables the teacher to give more individual attention to each pupil's learning needs.

- It allows pupils to become more actively involved in their own learning and to participate more freely in discussions. Students tend to participate more actively in small group situations.

- The method can be used in schools employing a variety of class arrangements, groupings, and schedules.
- It provides opportunities to develop respect for other students whose work helps the group progress in reaching its goals.

SOME DISADVANTAGES
The following are often mentioned as disadvantages of the group investigation strategy:

- The strategy is not supported by any specific research.
- Group projects often involve only the abler students, because these students are more capable of directing their own learning.
- The strategy sometimes requires different seating arrangements, different kinds of materials, and different kinds of teaching styles.
- The classroom setting does not always provide the best physical environment for small group study; the close proximity of groups to each other or to students studying independently can make for much interference.
- The success of the method depends on the ability of students to lead groups or to work independently.

CLASSROOM EXAMPLE (ELEMENTARY)
In this upper elementary open-space pod, the children are involved in group investigation activities related to a general study of Japan. Each group has selected a particular aspect of Japan that its members want to know more about. Three groups are meeting together, while two others are working on their own, using resource materials provided on carts in the center of the carpeted area.

The teacher is with one of the groups, assisting them in the development of their plans, while her aid is working with another. The teacher is reviewing with the small group the comments that she had made the previous day to the total class about the basic steps in group investigation. These children have selected a chairman for their group, but they are having difficulty in agreeing on procedures for moving ahead with their study. The teacher asks them to review the four stages of a group investigation—planning, gathering information, organizing information, and summarizing. The children find it difficult to decide on the course of action most likely to accomplish the goals of the group. The teacher suggests that they list on a piece of paper all the different things they want to learn about their topic, "Japanese Customs." When this is done, she asks the children to list possible sources for getting answers to these questions. They agree that they should have enough sources in the room and library to begin. She then suggests that the children think about which questions each would like to investigate, either on his own or with another member of the group, and let the chairman know. The teacher then moves from this group to another, to check on its progress.

In the next group, the students have completed their plans and are going through materials that the teacher had provided them for their topic, "Japanese Folk Tales." The chairman reports that the children have decided to each read several folk tales of Japan and then to come together again to talk about how these stories reflect the culture of the Japanese people. Their conclusions will be reported back to the class, along with the dramatization of one folk tale that illustrates their findings. The teacher compliments them on how well they are proceeding with their study.

The teacher leaves this group and goes over to an individual child who is sitting at the library table looking out the window, with a reference book in front of him. She asks if she can be of assistance, and he explains that he is unable to find what he needs in the encyclopedia. She assists him in using the index and leaves when he has found the information needed to complete his part of the group project.

As the time alloted to group work comes to an end, the teacher asks for everyone's attention. She then invites each chairman to give a brief report of progress, before moving on to the next activity.

Analysis/Comment (Elementary)
Because group investigation is a process that usually extends over a period of several days or

weeks or even longer, the classroom example that you just read only revealed a segment of the total picture. Let us look at the competency worksheet, however, and discuss the part that we were able to see in this open-space learning environment and what we did not see.

It is possible that these elementary students had never participated in any group investigation—possible, but unlikely, particularly since this school was built to accommodate the use of teaching strategies that involved individuals and small groups. Before beginning, however, the teacher did review the skills and procedures needed by the groups for investigating the topics that they selected. This review took place on the day before the visit that is described in the example. Most likely the discussion in class helped the teacher to gain a better understanding of how much the students knew about group investigation and how much experience they had had with this strategy before.

The teacher obviously did a very effective job of motivating the children to want to investigate Japan and to select topics of interest to them that were related to this unit of work. Most of the children were actively involved in their group studies, and although the first group that she talked with was having difficulty, its members still wanted to go ahead with their work together. They merely seemed to be in need of some help from the teacher in order to move ahead. She worked with this group long enough to leave its members with a sense of direction for their work. As she moved on to the second group, she often looked around the room to see how the other groups were proceeding. She gave the first group that she worked with special attention as she supervised the activities of her pupils.

The second group had moved along very well with the development of their plans, and they appeared to need only some positive reactions from their teacher. This she gave them through her thoughtful listening and her praise for their good work. The student leadership was particularly effective in this group.

The teacher's final contact, in this classroom example, is with the child working alone on an assignment that he had been given in his group. He appeared to be lost. It may be that he did not know how to use the encyclopedia, or perhaps he was not interested in pursuing the topic for which he had taken responsibility. Whatever the reason, the teacher went over to him and assisted him in using the index. An important point is that she did not leave until he had found what was needed for his part in the group study.

None of the groups observed in this classroom example had reached the point where the teacher seemed overly concerned about its progress. Because it was only the second day of the study, she accepted the fact that the groups would differ in abilities and would proceed at different rates in their studies. The second group had made exceptional progress. The members of the first group that she worked with, however, will probably need her help throughout their study together.

The final three checkpoints on the competency worksheet could be observed in this classroom only as the groups gather more information and begin to draw conclusions from it. Most likely the teacher has encouraged the students to be as creative as possible in selecting a manner for presenting their findings to the class. Media such as video and audio recorders, overhead transparency projectors, and slide projectors—increasingly available in elementary schools—could be effectively used for group presentations to the other pupils.

The teacher appeared to feel comfortable with the group investigation strategy and indicated through her actions that she understood the fact that she was not only developing understandings about Japan but also important group skills needed for effective living in a democratic society.

CLASSROOM EXAMPLE (SECONDARY)

A twelfth-grade physical education and health teacher who served as a school's tennis coach also used the group investigation strategy. Knowing that his tennis squad would probably be at the bottom of the league once again during the coming season, he determined to find ways to improve the situation. During the fall, he called a meeting of all returning varsity and junior varsity players. After explaining his interest in gaining league respectability, he asked for a sharing of the players' feelings. The unanimous interest in improving team, and individual, performance opened up for the teacher the opportunity to suggest that a group be formed to undertake a systematic investigation of the problem of how to improve team performance. At this time, the coach stated his willingness to try with the team the solution that the students' findings recommended. Through student volunteering, player recommendations, and the teacher's guidance, three boys were selected to comprise the group. All students were invited to feed ideas and observations into this investigative group, which was charged with reporting back to the teacher and the rest of the students just before the start of spring practice, some seven months later. The coach then checked student understanding of the task by asking a series of questions of the large group (which included the three special investigators).

With the consent of the teacher, the group decided to pursue its investigation in the P.E.-Health class that all three members attended, throughout fall "ladder" tennis matches, and also in the community in general. In class, the three students, with teacher supervision, studied the muscles of the body and developed exercises for strengthening those most related to the sport of tennis. During the fall matches, they analyzed the effects of various types and amounts of quick-energy foods, such as honey and oranges, or of having nothing at all during the course of a match. Community research involved talking with a dentist who used hypnosis and evaluating the desirability of using this to affect self-concept and physical performance in adolescents; for example, tennis players.

Throughout the work of the group, the teacher functioned entirely as "staff." In essence, he served as a consultant, a nondirective advisor. The school tennis courts, and health and physical education hardware and software were made available for group use as authorized and/or supervised by the teacher. At various times, he did ask for progress reports and also for a synthesis of what the group had achieved from its work. Based on the first of these reports, he authorized class credit for the project, even though the preliminary findings from the information coming in to him indicated no "cure-all" solution was going to be found.

Before the agreed-on time for the final report, the teacher and the investigative group met to discuss what conclusions could accurately be drawn from the investigation and how the report would be given. Then all prospective team members were called together. The report to this group, by one student who was selected by the investigative trio, emphasized a plan of action the group should follow to improve overall team performance. The plan included a sequence of exercise drills to be followed before each practice, authorized use of a high-energy beverage for rinsing out players' mouths during matches, and a program of tennis movies scheduled several times during the season to maintain images in the players' minds of effective ways to move and hit.

The "affirmative action" plan was agreed to by the players and was put into operation with the coach helping to facilitate and supervise. At the end of the season, unfortunately, the team had not improved its record and was encouraged by the league to drop out and enter a conference more compatible with the skill level of its players. Nonetheless, the students and the coach-teacher agreed that the group investigation and the ensuing application of its findings had been worth the time and effort.

Analysis/Comment (Secondary)

Here is a different twist to the employment of an instructional strategy! In this case, the "classroom" in which it is operating is not only the school and its facilities but also the community at large. The evident recognition by this teacher that learning is not confined to formal classroom settings is to be applauded. Moreover, in this example, note the use of a strategy in other areas of the curriculum—extra-curricular activities and physical education. One of the dominant truths about instructional strategies is their versatility for numerous situations calling for the systematic investigation of a research problem.

Other relatively uncommon but noteworthy observations about this use of the group investigation strategy are that it was carried out by just one small group of three students and that it was planned to continue for over two-thirds of a school year. And why not? Not all students in a teacher-student professional relationship need to be working through the same strategy at the same time. Then, too, investigative groups work well with three to four members. Science teachers in one high school report satisfactory results from investigative groups working together for as long as two years, so certainly six to seven months present no innate hang-up. Further, the project was open-ended. No "right" answer was known, not even by the teacher who was willing to listen to student recommendations and to apply them as warranted.

The teacher-coach presumably felt comfortable with his approach (application of the checkpoints could tell us more accurately) and he definitely allowed his students freedom to pursue their own learning and alternative solutions to a problem. With his background in coaching tennis and his status as a coach, he was in a position to encourage students to take on such a research project in the first place, one recognized by them as being important to explore. He checked to be sure the job was clear to students, and he served as both a materials and ideas resource for them.

Also on the "attending" side of his use of the strategy, it can be said that the task itself, and the concurrent freedom of students to choose group leaders as needed and to investigate on their own, probably aided these three students to become more self-sufficient—as the requirements of progress reports and synthesis probably contributed to helping them continually evaluate their efforts. The role the teacher chose for himself permitted him to offer guidance through process comments on qualities of leadership being shown in the group, ways of coping with frustration, procedures to facilitate intra-group cooperation and management/maintenance concerns, ways of determining the relative value and feasibility of undertaking selected procedures in trying to reach a goal, and ways of evaluating the effectiveness of small group efforts. The teacher is also seen in the example as making himself available to supervise student work, at least in the classroom aspect of their efforts. This, too, put him on more solid ground for helping students analyze their data, draw conclusions, and present their report—all of which he attends to in the example.

Should this teacher apply the complete list of checkpoints to his own performance, he would have to note that he gave no actual help to students in analyzing the processes of group dynamics or procedures for group investigation. No specific dates were worked out, no resources were specifically identified, nor were objectives agreed on, except for the general one of finding out how to improve team performance. The teacher would need to rethink his objective for selecting the strategy to see if he had planned to incorporate these skills and forgot, or whether he had not planned to use them, either because the students did not need such help or because he was not aware as to whether they did or not. In addition, the teacher made no estimate nor check of whether these students were capable of handling the skills necessary for group investigation: Do they have a knowledge of simple statistics, for instance? Except for agreeing on types of feedback (as progress reports) and an overall deadline (spring for the full report), he just basically "jumped in." Again, use of the checkpoints could remind the teacher of the aspect of conducting the full strategy through a gradual immersion, especially if students have had little experience with group investigation.

Although the conclusion of the example is not the outcome obviously desired, this teacher did give students the opportunity to try. He did not close out the investigation when success in terms of the immediate product of a higher league standing seemed doubtful, probably because the progress and learning seemed to him to be positive, even if the special outcome was not. It is quite probable that students working in the fashion described in the example will be able to function similarly in more regular classroom situations; that is, they could do group investigations. Our hope is that the teacher can also apply the strategy elsewhere, that he can see the many possibilities for using it in his physical education and health classes, and that he can use the strategy worksheet (as well as the rest of what is available on this current instructional strategy) to help himself if he chooses to employ group investigation in other aspects of his professional teaching.

NOTES

1. Lionel Tiger, *Men in Groups* (New York: Random House), pp. 93-125.

2. Seymour B. Sarason, *The Culture of the School and the Problem of Change* (Boston: Allyn and Bacon, 1971), p. 197.

3. Kenneth Rehage, *Social Studies in the Elementary Schools* (Washington, D.C.: National Council for the Social Studies, 1962), pp. 187-196.

4. Robert L. Ebel (ed.), *Encyclopedia of Educational Research* (New York: Macmillan Co., 1969), pp. 567-568.

5. Allan H. Glatthorn, "Small-Group Instruction," *Encyclopedia of Education*, Vol. 8 (New York: Macmillan Co. and Free Press), p. 230.

EVERETT LIBRARY QUEENS COLLEGE
CHARLOTTE, NORTH CAROLINA

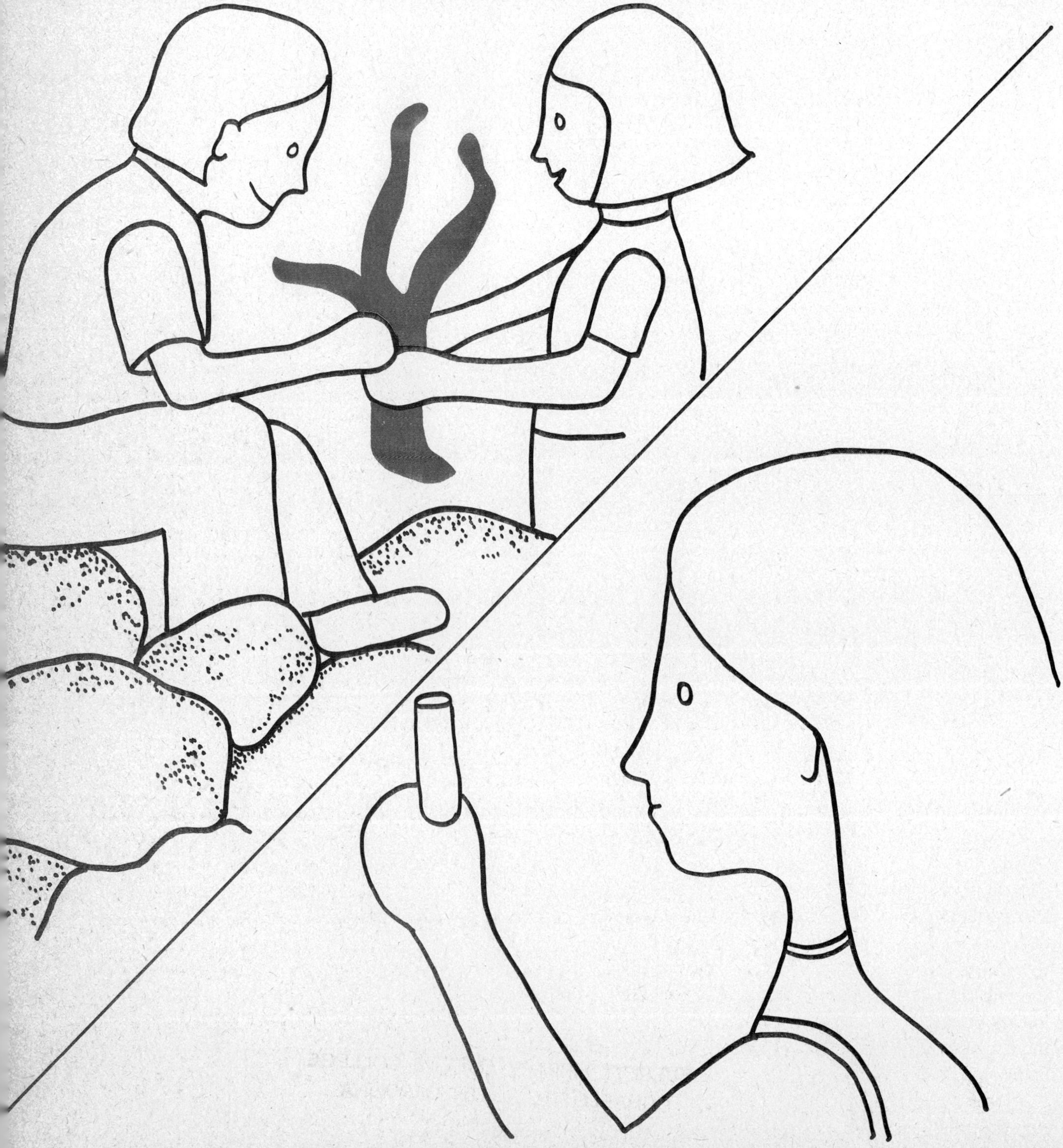

strategy 6

Laboratory Approach

BACKGROUND

Each of you who has been involved in the study of science at the high school or college level has most likely experienced the strategy of teaching commonly known as the laboratory approach. It is possible that for some of you science may have been the only course in which this strategy was used. It need not have been.

The laboratory approach is defined as the instructional procedure by which the cause, effect, nature, or property of any phenomenon—whether social, psychological, or physical—is determined by actual experience or experiment, under controlled conditions. You can readily see that this definition of the laboratory approach could be applied to curriculum areas other than science.

Pestalozzi (1746-1827), the Swiss educator who is given credit for developing the laboratory approach to teaching, certainly had more than science in mind when he formulated a philosophy of education that stressed that "education must proceed largely by doing instead of by words; the method of learning must be analytical; real objects and ideas must precede symbols and words." Pestalozzi's philosophy was greatly influenced by the social theorist Rousseau, whose book entitled *Emile* presented new ideas concerning the education of children when it was published in 1762.[1]

In practicing his philosophy, Pestalozzi revolutionized the methods and the subject matter in elementary schools; he is often referred to as the father of modern educational practice. For example, in teaching geography he would take children on walks, so that they would become more conscious of their environment. He used clay models to portray mountains and rivers' courses. In mathematics, he started with nonabstract objects, because he believed that abstractions can be understood only after concrete ideas have been mastered.[2]

One hundred years after Pestalozzi's death, more and more American teachers in a variety of fields were recognizing the value of his approach to teaching, which was generally referred to as the "laboratory method." In practicing this method, teachers had begun to do one or both of the following: (1) introduce some form of reality into their lessons—exhibits, models, products, and the like; and (2) carefully plan a series of direct instruction similar to a laboratory manual for the pupils' activities, which led to a solution of a problem under the guidance of a teacher.[3]

In any modern school, elementary or secondary, you will still see many examples of the laboratory method in action—although the teachers do not always refer to them by this name. Whenever a teacher is using objects to enhance instruction, assisting students in conducting an experiment, or taking children on a field trip, he is using the laboratory method. This method is the major strategy of instruction for industrial arts, vocational education, physical education, home economics, and, of course, science. It is also used in foreign language teaching and in outdoor education at both the elementary and secondary levels. Whatever the setting, the laboratory approach is based on the assumption that direct experience with materials, involving observation and participation, is superior to other methods for reaching the identified objectives.[4]

Research completed early in this century revealed evidence quite favorable to the laboratory approach. However, because the laboratory method can be practiced in a variety of ways and because the details of procedure vary so much in the studies, it is difficult to be definite about the outcomes of more recent research. The existing literature, however, does suggest that effective provisions can be made for individual differences and for socializing experiences through this method, if the teacher is sufficiently skillful and resourceful.[5]

The Handbook on Research in Teaching, in a discussion of the use of the laboratory method in science education with post-secondary students, states that—from the standpoint of theory—the activity of the student, the sensorimotor nature of the experience, and the individualization of laboratory instruction should cause the laboratory approach to contribute positively to learning. The author points out, however, that one would not expect laboratory teaching to have an advantage over other teaching methods in amount of information learned, but that one might expect the differences to be in retention, in ability to apply learning, or in actual skills in observation or manipulation of materials.[6]

Because of its sound theoretical base, the laboratory method continues to be popular for work with both young people and adults. Although research evidence has not been gathered to support it above other methods, those who have experienced it as teachers or students believe it has an important place in the ever-increasing list of strategies used by teachers.

COMPETENCY WORKSHEET FOR PLANNING AND OBSERVING

Checkpoints

Observer Notes

A teacher using the laboratory approach strategy can be observed performing the following behaviors:

_____ Clarifying the behavioral goals to be achieved by the students through the activity; e.g., experiment, field trip, demonstration.

_____ Selecting the appropriate resources for accomplishing these objectives; e.g., materials, equipment, selection of field trip location.

_____ Making plans that give consideration to all the details involved in the activity. (*Note:* This is especially important with a field trip, which often involves transportation, food, resource people, parent assistants, and a host of other details that can become problems if not given careful consideration prior to the trip.) For an experiment, planning might involve outlining in detail the steps to be followed.

_____ Checking out all the details of the plans by setting up and testing the equipment beforehand, conducting the experiment in private, or visiting the location of the field trip.

_____ Preparing the students for the activity by giving them a clear idea of expected outcomes; e.g., in a laboratory situation, this preparation might include a demonstration of the procedures involved. For a field trip, it might involve a review of how this activity relates to the unit of work being conducted in the classroom, what to look for, and how this information will be used when the students return to the classroom setting.

_____ Providing all students with the appropriate materials and equipment needed.

_____ Answering students' significant questions that are related to the activity and are essential to the attainment of the stated objectives of this experience, or having these questions answered by other resource people—e.g., a guide on a field trip.

_____ Raising significant questions during the activity, if these have not been asked by the students.

_____ Restating or clarifying points that appear to be unclear to the students.

_____ Facilitating a meaningful discussion following the activity.

_____ Assisting students in summarizing and evaluating what they have gained from this experience.

SOME ADVANTAGES
The following are often mentioned as advantages of the laboratory approach strategy:

- It allows for direct involvement by the learner, because the method emphasizes direct experience with materials pertinent to the area of study.

- It provides a multi-sensory approach, which provides for individual learning styles; e.g., students can often see, feel, smell, hear, and even taste objects involved, when the laboratory approach is used.

- It provides the student with a feeling of competence as he develops skills in the use of the materials involved, conducts an experiment, or explores a new environment.

- The strategy promotes a socializing atmosphere for students and teachers as they work together; e.g., in a laboratory setting or on a field trip.

- It provides opportunities for a more relevant curriculum, because the experiences provided often develop understandings and skills that can be used outside of the school setting.

- The method's use can develop skills necessary for more advanced study or research.

SOME DISADVANTAGES
The following are often mentioned as disadvantages of the laboratory approach strategy:

- It requires a very knowledgeable teacher, who can function in a setting where many diverse questions are being asked by the students.

- It can be distracting to students, because of the many activities that often take place simultaneously when this strategy is used.

- Information cannot be obtained as rapidly by direct experience or the trial and error of the laboratory setting as it can be obtained from abstractions presented orally or in print.

- The strategy requires careful and thorough planning in order to be effective.

- It can be expensive, if commercial materials are needed.

- The effect of this strategy on retention, ability to apply learning, skill in observation, and skill in manipulation of materials has not been thoroughly researched.

- Use of the strategy often results in loss of time because of inefficient classroom management.

- The strategy necessitates that a sufficient number of objects or specimens be made available, and this is often beyond the means of the school.

- Field trips are often viewed by administrators and parents as frill activities rather than as opportunities to see and do things that will provide significant learnings for students.

CLASSROOM EXAMPLE (ELEMENTARY)
Because of the careful planning needed for the effective use of the laboratory method, the field trip plan of a teacher in training was select-

ed as the classroom example for this strategy. Another reason for including the following plan is to illustrate how the "Competency Worksheet" can be used for planning as well as observing.

Plan for Field Trip to Embassy of Israel[7]

Grade 5—Social Studies
1. Behavioral Objectives
   a. Using background knowledge acquired from previous study and using prepared questions, the student will be able to ask relevant and appropriate questions concerning Israel.
   b. Using field trip experiences, the student will be able to describe in a discussion what was learned, what was seen, and opinions formulated from the experiences of visiting the Embassy of Israel.
2. Materials
   a. Guide for the planning of study trips, list for health and safety precaution, list for standards of courtesy and protection of property, instruction sheets for parents, principal's list of children going and staying, time schedule, attendance role, permission slips, thank-you card made by students, lesson plan, checklist for discussion.
3. Procedures
   a. Before the field trip
      1. Secure administrative approval for field trip to Embassy of Israel.
      2. Secure approval from Embassy of Israel.
      3. Secure parental approval for each child.
      4. Set up a time schedule for entire period of trip and mail to embassy. Have children take copies home to parents.
      5. Make arrangements for transportation.
      6. Ask students to pack a lunch.
      7. Find parents who will volunteer to accompany the group on the trip.
      8. Make a list of names, telephone numbers, and addresses of those children who are going and not going on the trip. Give both to the principal.
      9. Make plans and provisions for the children not going on the trip and give to principal.
      10. Discuss the following with the group:
          a. Purpose of trip.
          b. Safety precautions.
          c. Time schedule.
          d. Travel arrangements.
          e. Appropriate dress.
          f. Lunch plans.
          g. Standards of behavior.
          h. Procedures to follow during trip.
          i. Questions to ask guide.
   b. Day of field trip
      1. Pack extra lunches.
      2. Give each parent volunteer a list of students in his or her group, a time schedule, lunch plans, instruction sheets for standards and regulations set up for the children.
      3. Introduce each parent to children in his or her group.
      4. Check students' health.
      5. Take attendance on the bus.
      6. Allow each child to go to the restroom and to get a drink before leaving.
      7. Check to see if lunches have been brought. Give lunches to children who have forgotten.
      8. Upon arrival at embassy, children will unload in an orderly manner and enter embassy in groups with parent.
      9. During visit, children will ask questions.
      10. After visit, class will eat lunch in the park.
      11. After lunch, return to school.
   c. After the field trip
      1. Thank bus driver and parents.
      2. Get children who did not go and return to class.
      3. In class, have children write a thank-you card to the embassy guide.
      4. After card is finished, lead a follow-up discussion and sharing-time on trip. For example, allow one or two children to share what occurred with those who did not go on trip. Ask questions such as: What impressed you the

most? Do you believe it was a worthwhile trip? What misconceptions did you have that were clarified on the trip?
4. Evaluation
   a. The student will be evaluated by the teacher on the type of questions asked during the visit.
   b. The student will be evaluated by the teacher on the follow-up discussion and sharing-time.

Analysis/Comment (Elementary)
Let us review the plan of the future teacher to see how well it follows the checkpoints on our list.

First, the teacher has clarified the behavioral goals to be achieved by the children through this field trip to the Embassy of Israel. Although it is difficult to truly know what the expected outcomes might be for each student, because there can be a variety of incidental learnings, she has indicated in her plan that she would like the students to use and build on their previous learnings about Israel as they visit the official embassy in Washington, D.C. The plan does not indicate what the pupils will see. However, one assumes, that, since the teacher has contacted the embassy and made arrangements with the officials there, she has also discussed in detail what the students might see and do on their visit. She has obviously selected a trip to the Embassy of Israel because she believes it will provide an opportunity worth the time and effort involved.

Her plan for the trip is quite detailed. She has listed what needs to be done before the field trip, on the day of the field trip, and after the trip. She has given consideration to securing administrative approval and parental approval. She has established a time schedule for the trip and has sent this home with a note to the parents that also included additional information about the need for each child to bring his own lunch and drink. In addition she has made arrangements for any children who might not be able to go on the field trip and has given lists of those who are and are not going to the principal. She has also found parents who can accompany the group on the trip.

There is no indication in her plan that she has actually visited the Embassy of Israel, but it is usually a wise idea to visit the field trip site beforehand if possible. This gives the teacher a better idea of what the site has to offer, so that she can better prepare the children for the experience.

Continuing along the list of checkpoints, note that the teacher has planned a session for discussing with the children the purpose of the trip and other related matters. Of major importance is the fact that she has included time for children to think together about some of the questions that they might like to ask their guide. When possible, questions can be prepared ahead of time and mailed or telephoned to the field trip site for those who will be working with the teacher and the class.

The teacher's plan for the day of the trip reveals the careful and thorough planning needed to provide a safe and pleasurable learning experience. The teacher has thought through the various aspects of the trip that can be handled only on the day of the trip and has made careful plans to involve the volunteer parents with their groups as early in the day as possible. Naturally, the true success of the day will depend on the understandings gained from the actual visit to the embassy, but the teacher has made ample plans to ensure that all the details that are needed to contribute to the success of the total day have been considered. Hopefully, the visit provided a time for the questions that the children had developed to be asked. Other questions were probably inspired by the comments of the guide and by the setting.

The teacher's plan ends with the activities following the field trip, when the class is back at the school. In addition to the basic responsibilities listed in the plan, she also includes a discussion period, during which she can help students to summarize and evaluate some of the learnings from their visit to the Embassy of Israel.

The final section of the plan indicates how she will evaluate the original behavioral objectives established at the beginning of the plan. This is always very difficult to do, but through her observations during the trip and during the discussion that follows, she should have a fairly good idea of how effective this use of the laboratory method was for the students in her class.

As you can see, the list of checkpoints could be followed very carefully in reviewing the plan of this young future teacher. Hopefully, each of the lists in this book can be of assistance to both future teachers and experienced teachers in their planning for this strategy as well as the others that are described.

CLASSROOM EXAMPLE (SECONDARY)

In this secondary example, the laboratory method was selected for use by a modified version of a teaching team. A third-period English teacher first thought of the idea as a way of presenting one of his emphases for the year; he discussed it with an agreeable colleague who taught music. Both had the same students, one period apart. Their thought was to have students develop a filmstrip-tape show in English class and the music class that followed. The theme of the work would relate to the year's plan in English for the class, and would be, specifically, "A Study of Film" unit. It was agreed by the teachers and by the students to whom the idea was presented that the finished product would be presented in all interested classes as well as to an upcoming P.T.A. session.

Before the unit began, the teachers did what they could to collect films representative of eras in the movie industry as well as to obtain references on the history of film. The music teacher, particularly, researched songs that had been played in theaters to accompany silent films. When the unit got under way, students had a continuous two-period involvement. In the English class, they watched the films and discussed techniques used with the teacher. When it was agreed that a technique was representative of a particular era of film-making, the students staged a "model" of that technique and "shot" it with the school camera. For instance, they practiced with the still photography devices of altering an object through lighting, photographing someone in perhaps six different moods to get the shot wanted—an approach that exemplified a specific characteristic in film history. (Illustrating "slap-stick" brought much laughter and one parent demanding to know: "Is this *English?*") The English teacher, in whose room most of this work was done, moved from student to student and group to group, to be sure students were clear on what they were about and how the different techniques they were investigating and duplicating affected "product."

Developing photographs was another job of the students. A darkroom of sorts was fashioned in a corner of the classroom and, with some help from the teacher, students developed, dried, and labeled in sequence the shots they wanted to compose the filmstrip. Because not all students could work at one time on film development but all were asked to find out the secrets of this aspect of photography, other members of the class viewed and listened to filmstrip-tape presentations from the NEA and additional professional sources. Their work included making a list of hints for producing a quality filmstrip-tape show, such as the minimum amount of time a frame should normally be held before a viewer. To make this list, careful analysis was necessary. In effect, these students had to break down a filmstrip-tape production and build up one of their own. The school audio-visual consultant served as a resource, helping them figure out how to make a filmstrip from a series of photographs. (Job opportunities were rotated, then, as the darkroom became available.) Scriptwriting was also investigated, through use of the "texts" for the unit. Students were asked to write a script on the history of film, to which optical and sound effects could be added. Small group work on this project was planned and carried out. The English teacher asked students, in the course of doing the writing, what criteria they used to select items for inclusion in the final script. This question led into a discussion of selective editing and how what we see and hear from a medium is only part of a total experience.

In music class, under the direction of the teacher, students had the main project of creating a musical score that would lead in to the body of the presentation, underscore it, and "fade out" at the end of the presentation. This project required analyses of sounds made by different instruments and investigation of how the rhythms of language and music can be correlated to set certain sounds to a particular picture. Interestingly, as a by-product of testing the properties of a variety of musical instruments, students found a sound cue that would serve appropriately on the tape for helping the projectionist know when to change frames. They also collected sounds at different locations in the building (and outside), analyzed these in terms of such musical qualities as pitch, intensity, and tone-color, and experimented with their effectiveness in conveying a message on the tape. Again, the teacher was available to answer questions, redirect thinking, or suggest ideas, so that students could determine answers for themselves.

Toward the end of the unit, students had to work out the recording of the tape and the synchronization of the tape with the filmstrip. The school audio-visual consultant was again brought in to advise the students as they worked in achieving a finished production. The completed filmstrip-tape show was viewed by the students themselves, prior to its getting any "outside" exposure. After this, the teachers held a final open and far-reaching discussion with the students, which confirmed their belief that the laboratory method used in this unit had served them all quite well.

Analysis/Comment (Secondary)
Although both teachers used the laboratory method in this example—and used it rather inclusively to enable student learning—they nowhere clearly stated the behavioral goals of the lesson. Rather, they have assumed that the students would be interested in a project that came to the attention of the English teacher. It is well to give benefit of doubt, and most students would probably be interested in producing a filmstrip-tape show. However, the checklist, if used, would tend to help both teachers and observers remember and adhere to those specific teacher behaviors that go to make up a given instructional strategy, including the behavior of stating goals. As another point, such early and continuing attention to objectives would help when the teachers must account to the parent who asked how the study of films is "English." This would be what the checklist calls a "significant question related to the activity." It could come from a parent, as in the example, or from a student. In either event, the professional teacher should have a sound answer.

To the credit of the teachers in the example, they did select appropriate resources for accomplishing what they seemed to be after. And they did seem to give sufficient attention to the administrative details involved with teaching through the laboratory method. For example, to supplement their own knowledge and give the students aid in their endeavors, they booked in advance films as well as the school A-V consultant. Whether the teachers fully tested out their plans —for example, the making of a filmstrip—beforehand is doubtful. Doing so would help ensure learning and, hence, the item is appropriately on the checklist. Without attention to advance testing, students could be enthusiastic about a project, time and details could be arranged, and yet the project could collapse—because, for instance, no one realized that the amount of light getting into the room would ruin the negatives.

One other major point that it is well to note has to do with the observation that the teachers did not really prepare the students for the activities by giving them a clear idea of expected outcomes. The students had probably seen filmstrip-tape shows before, but it is doubtful they had thought much about the history of film as it reflects culture, or the use of music to convey mood and message, or how selective editing influences product and, subsequently, audience. Previewed outcomes such as these would give students a sense of where they are headed and what to look for along the way.

Finally, in terms of the checklist, it may be observed that at least one "significant question" is raised by the teacher—that dealing with the processes of selective editing. In addition, the teachers are consistently available to restate or clarify for students. Moreover, the concluding discussion offers opportunity for meaningful review of what has been gained from the experience.

It would seem, judging from this classroom episode, that during the production of the filmstrip-tape show, the use of the laboratory method in part—as in the "photography" and "musical synchronization" aspects of the example—and in whole provided direct experiences with materials and involved pupil observation and participation to facilitate personal learning. In sum, the instructional strategy is here appropriately selected and represents yet another teaching maneuver available to aid teachers achieve their professional goals.

NOTES

1. Martin J. Stormzard, *Progressive Methods of Teaching* (Boston: Houghton-Mifflin, 1927), p. 201.

2. Frederick Mayer, *A History of Educational Thought* (Columbus, Ohio: Charles E. Merrill, 1960), pp. 266-267.

3. Martin J. Stormzard, *op. cit.*, p. 231.

4. Norman E. Wallen and Robert M. W. Travers, "Analysis and Investigation of Teaching Methods," *Handbook of Research on Teaching* (Chicago: Rand McNally, 1963), p. 483.

5. G. Max Wingo, "Methods of Teaching," *Encyclopedia of Educational Research* (New York: Macmillan Co., 1960), p. 851.

6. W. J. McKeachie, "Research on Teaching at the College and University Level," *Handbook of Research on Teaching* (Chicago: Rand McNally, 1963), pp. 1144-45.

7. Adapted from lesson plan prepared by Ms. Bonnie Hobson for Education 402: Methods for Intermediate Grades, George Mason University, Spring 1974.

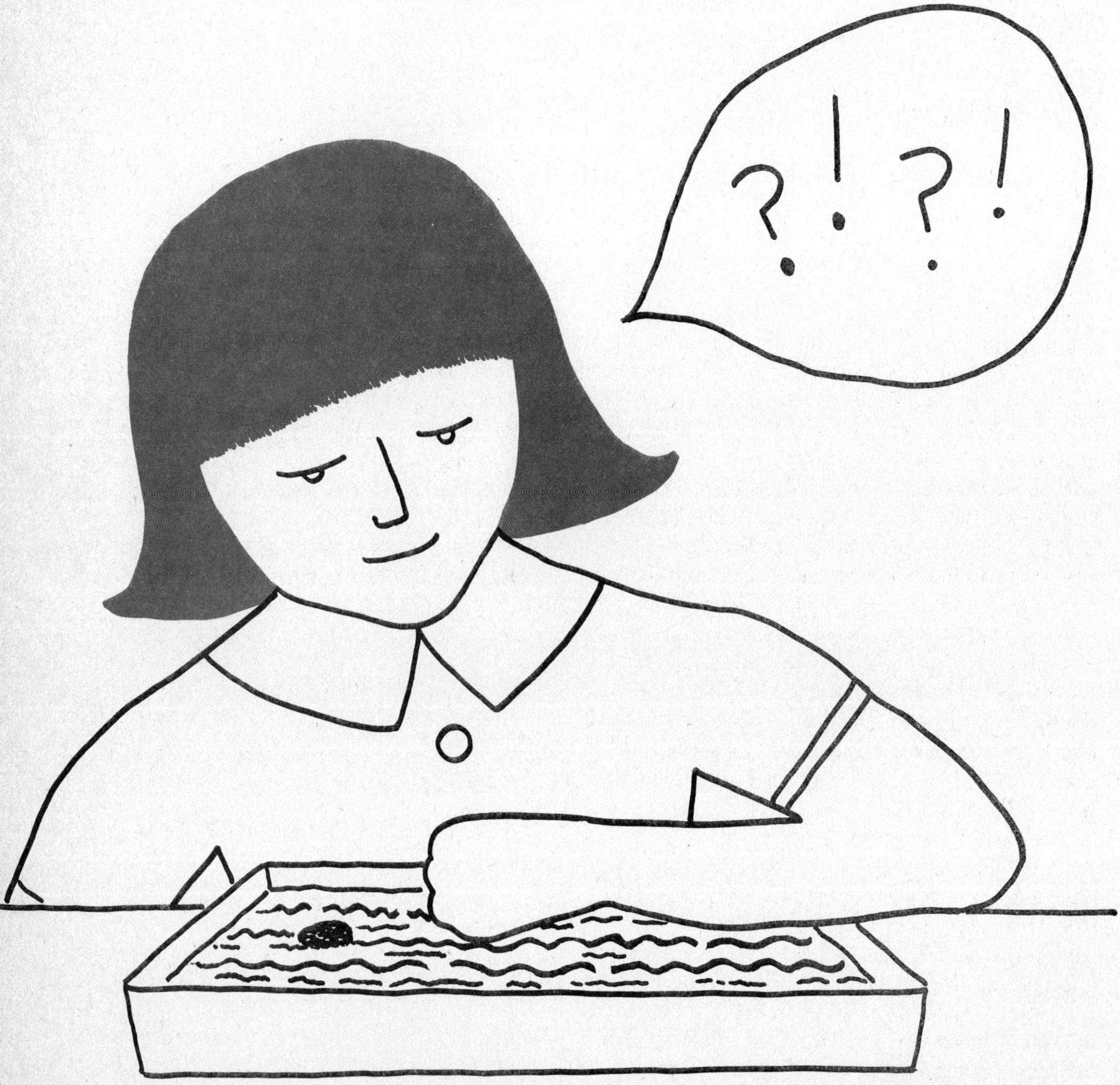

strategy 7

Discovery

BACKGROUND

The term *discovery method* is defined as a teaching procedure that emphasizes individual study, manipulation of objects, and other experimentation by the student before generalizations are made; the method requires delay in verbalization of important discoveries until the student is aware of a concept. The discovery method is a component of a division of educational practice that is often referred to as "heuristic" teaching, a type of teaching that includes methods designed to promote a broad range of active, process-oriented, self-directed, inquiring, and reflective modes of learning.[1] Several of the other strategies included in this book would also be considered to be directly related to heuristic teaching, if they are used in a manner that stimulates the student to investigate further by himself without the aid of the teacher; i.e., laboratory approach, independent study.

The current educational literature for teachers seems unnecessarily confusing when the discovery method is discussed. Perhaps this is caused by the fact that the title of this strategy appears to tell the total story. One might conclude that the discovery approach is one in which teachers allow students to discover, on their own, information that in traditional settings they would have been told. Such a simplistic analysis, however, only reveals one layer of a strategy that is much more complex.

In practice, teachers use the discovery approach along a line that ranges from guided discovery to unguided discovery, with each point along the way defined by the amount of guidance given by the teacher. Add to this picture the fact that the students may approach the achievement of educational objectives in both structured and unstructured manners at any point on this line, and you can see the complexity of the discovery method.

We had hoped to be able in this section to simplify and clarify the discovery approach, but in our research we "discovered" the following points of confusion about the strategy:

Discovery is often used interchangeably with *inquiry* and *problem-solving*.

Some educators see distinct differences between *discovery* and *inquiry*.

Others see *discovery* as a subcategory of *inquiry*.

Others see *inquiry* as a subcategory of *discovery*.

Others write about heuristic modes that include *discovery* and *inquiry*.

For the purposes of this discussion, we have decided to follow the example of the respected *Encyclopedia of Educational Research* and to explore discovery as a unique strategy that can be structured by the teacher in several ways, including the teaching of the skills of inquiry and problem solving as tools for the student in his attainment of educational objectives.

Jerome Bruner, the Harvard psychologist and one of the more eloquent proponents of the discovery approach, would support this way of handling the section, we suspect, because he lists as one of the advantages of the strategy that "solving problems through discovery develops a style of inquiry or problem-solving that serves for any task—or almost any task—one may encounter."[2]

Bruner, by the way, is the person most closely associated with the discovery strategy; he has used it in the development of curriculum materials. Biehler points out, however, that the greatest influence during this century on the use of the discovery method was the work of John Dewey. Earlier in the century, Dewey was pointing to the limitations of teacher-directed learning and arguing that true education was much more than a transmission of information. He encouraged the development of the natural tendencies of the child, especially the tendency toward inquiry. His point of view was that school experiences should help students to learn how to *inquire* about things effectively instead of merely helping them to *acquire* learning.[3]

A review of the arguments and evidence on teaching by discovery reveals that guided discovery—giving the learner only some of the cues he needs—can be used in teaching some aspects of some subjects with advantages for learning, retention, and transfer.[4] Such a moderate position seems to be supported by both research and common sense, and it underlies our selection of guided discovery as the basis for the competency worksheet on this current instructional strategy.

The discovery method is now used in many curriculum programs—the "new math," for instance—where developing generalizations by means of discovery is replacing teacher-prescribed ways of operating with numbers. It is also commonly used in disciplines such as social studies and English for teaching students about the nature of concepts, specific concepts themselves, and how to be more effective in forming and attaining concepts. (See Classroom Examples.)

In sum, even though confusion is associated with defining discovery, it deserves to be one of a number of instructional strategies that teachers should possess as they work to deal effectively with the different learning styles of different students.

COMPETENCY WORKSHEET FOR PLANNING AND OBSERVING

Checkpoints

Observer Notes

When using the guided discovery strategy, the teacher is usually observed performing the following behaviors:

_____ Assessing pupil need and interest and using the findings as a basis for determining useful and realistic subjects for discovery teaching.

_____ Preselecting, on the basis of pupil need and interest, an initial principle, generalization, concept, or relationship to be learned.

_____ Organizing physical arrangements in the teaching area

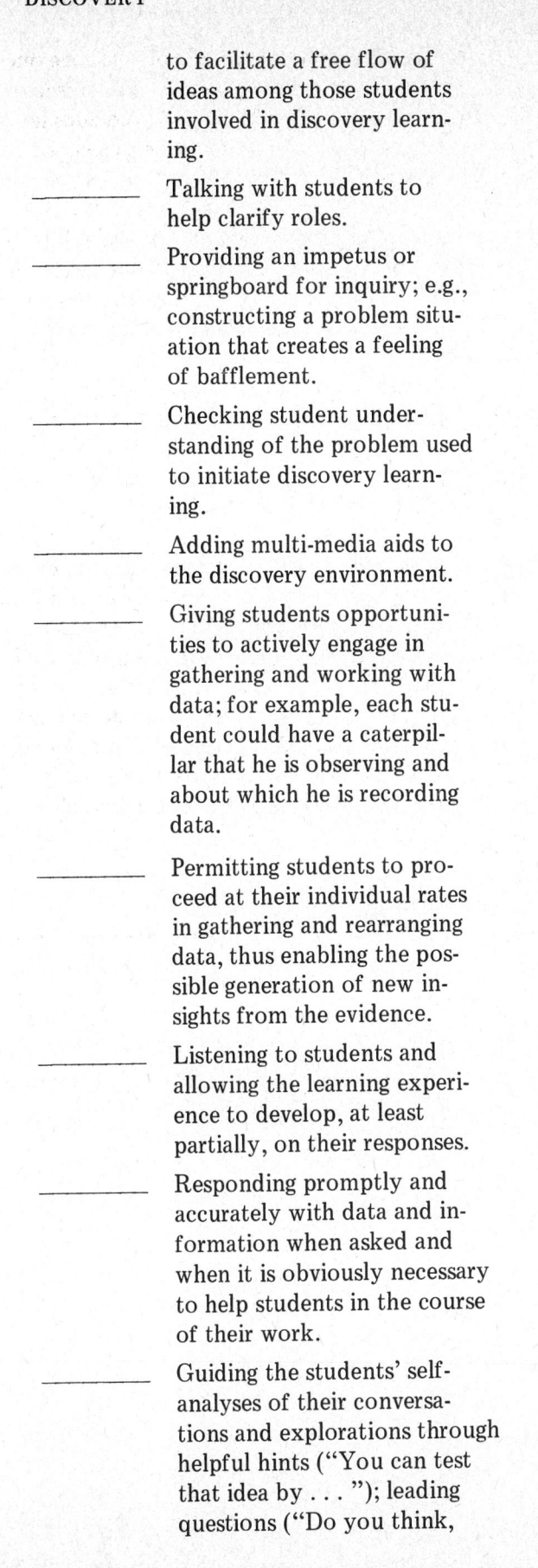

DISCOVERY

_____ to facilitate a free flow of ideas among those students involved in discovery learning.

_____ Talking with students to help clarify roles.

_____ Providing an impetus or springboard for inquiry; e.g., constructing a problem situation that creates a feeling of bafflement.

_____ Checking student understanding of the problem used to initiate discovery learning.

_____ Adding multi-media aids to the discovery environment.

_____ Giving students opportunities to actively engage in gathering and working with data; for example, each student could have a caterpillar that he is observing and about which he is recording data.

_____ Permitting students to proceed at their individual rates in gathering and rearranging data, thus enabling the possible generation of new insights from the evidence.

_____ Listening to students and allowing the learning experience to develop, at least partially, on their responses.

_____ Responding promptly and accurately with data and information when asked and when it is obviously necessary to help students in the course of their work.

_____ Guiding the students' self-analyses of their conversations and explorations through helpful hints ("You can test that idea by . . . "); leading questions ("Do you think, perhaps, that you are starting off with a 'solution' and skipping some of the preliminary steps in solving the problem?"); and identification of processes used ("I notice you've organized your data by plotting it on a graph.").

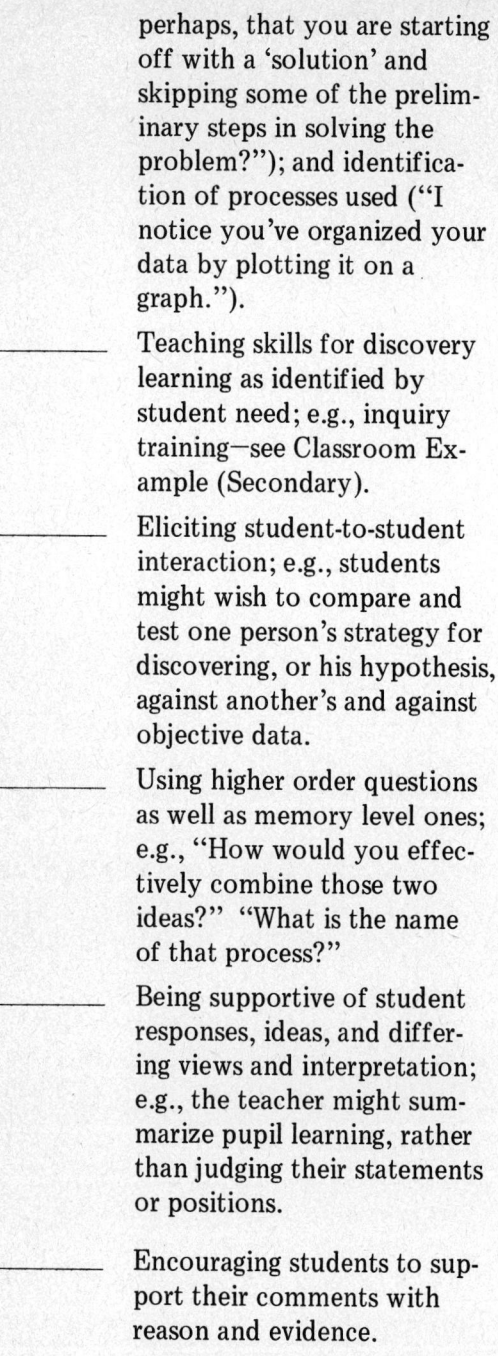

_____ Teaching skills for discovery learning as identified by student need; e.g., inquiry training—see Classroom Example (Secondary).

_____ Eliciting student-to-student interaction; e.g., students might wish to compare and test one person's strategy for discovering, or his hypothesis, against another's and against objective data.

_____ Using higher order questions as well as memory level ones; e.g., "How would you effectively combine those two ideas?" "What is the name of that process?"

_____ Being supportive of student responses, ideas, and differing views and interpretation; e.g., the teacher might summarize pupil learning, rather than judging their statements or positions.

_____ Encouraging students to support their comments with reason and evidence.

_____ Complimenting students who engage in the specific operations or processes of discovery; e.g., students who ask one another or the teacher questions of different levels, and students who identify the products of their own inquiry, as in: "I have a theory about . . ."

_____ Helping students write or verbalize the rule, principle, idea, generalization, or concept that was central to the original problem and that was "discovered" through this strategy.

_____ Checking to see if students show evidence of using what they have discovered (techniques and concepts, for example), in subsequent situations; for instance, situations in which students can choose their own approaches for solving their own problems. (This could be accomplished, for example, by the teacher making note of any increase in the frequency and variety of their inquiry skills.)

SOME ADVANTAGES
The following are often mentioned as some of the advantages of the discovery strategy:

- It is likely to help improve and/or increase the pupil's supply and control of cognitive skills and processes, provided he is involved consistently in guided discovery. Greater strength in the processes of discovery comes from trying to discover; in effect, one learns *how* to learn.

- Knowledge gained through this strategy is most uniquely personal and is probably the most powerful (in terms of depth of understanding, retention, and transfer, for example).

- The discovery strategy produces a sense of excitement in students. For example, they can get the sense of groping, exploring, succeeding, and occasionally failing that comes to all who inquire on their own (scientists, for instance).

- The method allows a student to move along paths best suited to his own abilities.

- It causes the student to direct much of his own learning, and thus he is likely to become ego-involved and more self-motivated for learning—at least on a particular discovery project.

- The method could help strengthen a student's self-concept as he gains confidence with the processes from working with them. This might allow, for example, a student to be more able to pursue causal relationships under highly frustrating conditions.

- The strategy is student-centered; for example, it allows students and teachers to participate as active equals where ideas are concerned. The teacher can become a fellow-learner, an investigator—especially in discovery situations where the "answer" is not known in advance.

- It aids the student's development of a healthy skepticism toward "final and ultimate" truths.

SOME DISADVANTAGES

The following are often mentioned as some of the disadvantages of the discovery strategy:

- It assumes a certain readiness of mind for this kind of learning. For example, slower students might be confused in attempting to do divergent thinking, deal with abstractions, find the interrelatedness of concepts within a subject, or compose what they find in either written or oral form. More intellectually able students might monopolize the discoveries, creating frustration for others.

- The method is not especially efficient for teaching large numbers of students. For example, a great deal of time could be spent helping just one student discover the theories of government upon which the Declaration of Independence is based, or discovering why certain words are spelled as they are.

- The expectations in the strategy can be disruptive to students and teachers who are accustomed to more traditional planning and teaching.

- Discovery teaching might be viewed by some as de-emphasizing the attainment of attitudes and skills in favor of gaining understandings, when attitudes and skills might well be required for achieving genuine understanding and/or furthering the overall social-emotional development of the child.

- In some disciplines (science, for example), the facilities needed for testing ideas might not be available.

- The strategy may not provide opportunities for creative thinking, some educators argue, since the concepts to be discovered are preselected by the teacher, and the processes are under his guidance.

CLASSROOM EXAMPLE (ELEMENTARY)

Bruner reports the following illustration of the discovery method.[5] The object of the lesson was to help students learn that, generally speaking, one can reduce a language into what is called type and order:

First write a sentence on the board. Then get children to form similar sentences as follows—

The	man	ate	his	lunch.
A	boy	stole	a	bike.
The	dog	chased	my	cat.
My	father	skidded	the	car.
A	wind	blew	his	hat.

At this particular point, we have the children provide other sentences ad libitum. And they provide them. Sometimes they are wrong. Usually not. We then shift them to the following puzzle: How is it that one can go from left to right across the sentences in practically any row and still come out with a sentence: The boy chased the cat; A father chased a lunch; The man stole my bike; A father stole his hat. Some of the sentences are rather silly, but clearly sentences. Soon they will say things like, "There are five places and you can put lots of things in each place." But which kinds of words will fit into each column? Type and token begin to emerge as ideas. Now we reach a very critical point. Ask, for example, whether they can make up some more columns. One child proposed the following, something that put the class on a new level of attitude toward the use of mind. He said that there is a "zero" column that could contain the word "did." I asked what other particular words this column could contain. The children said, "did," "can," "has." This was the zero column. Then one of the pupils said that this did not quite fit and that you would have to change the word in the third column, too, but it would not be very much of a change. They were ready and willing now to get into the syntax of the language, to invent it afresh. They talked about the family of words that would fit and that two columns affected the families each could carry. Only then did we introduce some terminology. We talked about type and order, and that in sentences there were words that were types and they appeared in a certain permissible order. One of the children said of types, "They're called parts of speech. A noun, for example, is a 'person, place or thing.'"

Analysis/Comment (Elementary)

This example of guided discovery with a group of elementary children illustrates the principles of inductive teaching that are usually characteristic of the discovery method. Although this is a very brief look at the discovery strategy in action, it was included as the elementary classroom example because it represents a description of the discovery approach to learning as reported by Jerome Bruner. In spite of its brevity, the example does contain enough teacher behaviors from our list of checkpoints that one can analyze the varous steps often taken in using the discovery strategy.

We assume that the teacher in the example has assessed the needs of his pupils and, on the basis of this review, has selected the generalization that language can be reduced to type and order as the understanding to be learned. The children have obviously participated in a session of this kind before, because they appear to understand the unique role of the teacher in the discovery approach and to feel comfortable when involved in this strategy.

The springboard for inquiry in the example is, of course, the sentence puzzle: "How is it that one can go from left to right across the sentences in practically any row and still come out with a sentence?" The teacher checks the students' understanding of this question by reviewing with them the sentences they have developed. Because the teacher has used a chalkboard as an aid in this discovery experience, the children are quickly able to grasp the problem that he has presented.

The teacher listened to the children's responses, accepting each as being important and worthwhile, and then he asked a question that raised their thinking to another level. The teacher asked, as you recall, whether or not they could "make up some more columns." He was very supportive of their responses, but he raised questions that would aid them in analyzing their comments and testing their ideas.

When it seemed appropriate to do so, he began to help the children verbalize what they were learning through the guided discovery experience, as he continued to raise questions that would lead them to a discovery and understanding of the generalization that was the focus of this learning experience. As this episode ends, the students have just about reached the point where they could formulate and verbalize the central concept, if the teacher were to ask them to do so. From the discovery procedure that the students and teachers went through, it is probable that the children will internalize both the broad concept of the importance of type and order in language and the process through which they gained it, and will be able to draw on both in future situations.

Without doubt, the discovery method, as this analysis points out, is worthy of employment and belongs in the professional teacher's repertoire along with other strategies for instruction.

CLASSROOM EXAMPLE (SECONDARY)

The following classroom example offers a sketch of a discovery lesson in science, during which the teacher is helping students use and expand their repertoire of inquiry skills.[6] Mention should be made that in the following example, the group with which the teacher is using what we have defined as the discovery strategy is called the "inquiry group."

Teacher Behavior

(1) The teacher worked with a group of twelve students on the inquiry activity, while a second group of twelve was watching a sound filmstrip related to the topic under study by the entire class; a third group of twelve was busy reading and carrying out some science investigations outlined in their textbook. The teacher began work with

Student Behavior

the "inquiry group" after the other groups were at work. He planned to rotate the groups on following days so that all students would have a chance to participate in all three activities.

(2) "Today I'm going to show you a kind of science experiment. Then I'll pose a question about it. It will be your job to see if you can figure out how it works or why it works the way it does. OK?"

(3) "One thing I'll ask you to do is to raise your hand if you want to say something or ask some questions."

(4) The teacher holds up a pulse glass, a four-inch tube formed in a *U* shape. A one-inch glass globe is attached to each end of the *U* of the tube. One of the glass globes is partially filled with a red liquid. As he holds it so that all can see, he places his hand around this globe. The red liquid moves to the uncovered globe. He then places his other hand on the filled globe and takes his hand away from the empty one. The red liquid now moves back into the uncovered globe.

(5) "One question you might want to think about is why the red liquid moves."

(6)   Mike: "Is this thing a thermometer?"

(7) "No."

(8)   Mike: "Does it work like a thermometer does?"

(9) "It might."

(10)   Mike: "Hmm."

(11)   Gina: "Do you squeeze it to make it go?"

(12) "When you say 'squeeze it,' Gina, do you mean am I pressing in on the glass?"

(13)   Gina: "Yeah, I mean are you holding it real tight in your hand when it goes?"

(14) "I'm holding it reasonably tight, but I'm not squeezing it real hard."

(15)   Gina: "Well, what makes it go, then?"

(16) "That is your job. It's up to you to figure out what makes it go."

(17)   Maria: "Your hand's warm and that makes it go."

(18) "Just a minute, Maria, I want to make sure that Gina is through. Gina, did you want to say anything else?"

(19)   Gina: "No."

(20) "OK, now it's your turn, Maria."

(21)   Maria: "Well, is it?"

(22) "Is what?"

(23)   Maria: "Is your hand warm?"

(24) "Do you want to touch my hand so you can decide? Find out if it's warm."

(25)   Maria: "Sure. It's warmer than mine. Your hand is warm. Will it work with cold hands?"

(26) "Do you want to try it to find out?"

(27)   Maria takes the pulse glass and holds one side of it. The red liquid remains at the same level for a moment, but then moves slowly to the uncovered side.

(28)   Maria: "Hey, it doesn't move as fast for me. Did you heat up your hand or something before you touched it?"

(29) "No, I didn't."

(30)   Mike: "Can I try it, too?"

(31) "Sure. Maria, when you're through, would you please pass it to Mike?"

(32)   Maria: "In a minute, Mike, I'm not finished with my experiment yet."

(33)   She places her other hand on the uncovered sphere and observes what happens. She turns the glass upside down and at several angles and observes the results.

(34)   Maria: "Hey, I can make it run uphill!"

(35)   Mike: "Let me try it now."

(36)   Maria passes the pulse glass to Mike. He places his hands over both spheres. The red liquid does not move. He then places his hand around the tube connecting the two spheres. The red liquid does not move. Finally he places his hand over one sphere and the liquid moves to the uncovered side.

(37)   Mike: "Is this stuff in here mercury?"

(38) "No, it isn't."

(39)   Mike: "What is it?"

(40) "Methyl alcohol."

(41)   Mike: "Methe...what?"

(42) "Methyl alcohol."

(43)

(44) "What would you like to use?"

(45)

(46) "No, it wouldn't work if you used water."

(47)

(48) "No, it's not the same."

(49)

(50) "Let me see if I understand you, Mike. You're saying the liquid in here expands—takes up more room—is that what you mean?"

(51)

(52) "Oh, you have a kind of heat theory or expansion theory about what makes it go. It's up to you to figure out if your theory is a good one."

(53)

(54) "What do you mean by 'cold place'?"

(55)

(56) "You mean if you were to do everything the same—put your hand over it just like I did—but you did it in a refrigerator, would it work the same?"

(57)

(58) "Yes, it would work the same."

(59) "OK, let's stop here for now. Before we go to lunch, let me ask what you think of what we have done today, and how you feel about it."

(60)

(61) "No. That's what inquiry is all about—learning how to decide for yourself if your answer is a good one."

(62)

Mike: "Well, could you use something else? Would it go with something else?"

Mike: "Water?"

Mike: "Is it the same stuff that's in thermometers? Ya' know, that red stuff?"

Mike: "Well, is that how it works? Does the stuff inside there expand when you heat it like a thermometer goes up when it gets hot?"

Mike: "Yeah, it gets bigger; you put your hand over it and the heat from your hand makes the red liquid get bigger so it has to take up more room and it moves to the other side."

Gina: "If you were to put it in some place real cold, would it work?"

Gina: "Like, if I could take it into a refrigerator, would it work there?"

Gina: "Yeah."

Gina: "Are you going to tell us the answer?"

Gina: "You mean you're not going to tell us?"

(63) "No, but I want to make it possible for you to work so you can tell for yourself."

(64)

Mike: "I think you wanted us to figure out the answers for ourselves rather than you telling us the answer. Is that what you want us to do?"

(65) "Yes, to learn how to figure out answers for yourselves. Do any of you feel that you do have a good theory?"

(66)

Frank: "Yes, I think it's heat."

(67) "How do you know your theory is a good one?"

(68)

Frank: "Because it is. When you put heat on it goes. Or when you take heat away with ice or something cold it goes the other way."

Analysis/Comment (Secondary)
This is a helpful example of the guided discovery strategy in operation. For example, in the opening description (1), the teacher makes the physical arrangements clear: Students will be divided into groups, and each group will have its own activity. Relationship to preceding lessons is not stated for the students, although such is most likely in the teacher's mind. It is often helpful to share this "tie-in" element with the class.

It is obvious, in the total example, that attention to process shares equal billing with solving a problem. This is supported by the observation (60-64) that the "right" answer has been available all along, thus further suggesting that the teacher's primary goal is really to help the students focus on the processes of inquiry. He confirms this himself (65). Although no check is made as to whether students are truly interested in concepts about heat, change of state and pressure, or skills of the inquiry process, these are not unlikely probablilities. In addition, the choice to begin this lesson with what is presumably a "puzzlement" to students—and this is substantiated by Gina (15)—along with the teacher's invitation to ask questions (3), implies teacher recognition of the needs, if not the interests, of the students.

The problem raised (4) seems to be a useful and interesting one for students learning the concept and skills involved. The teacher fosters initial inquiry for getting at the concept by simple structuring through directions to "raise your hand" (3) and hints such as, "One question you might want to think about is . . . ." (5). Other structuring moves helpful at this point might have been to make students aware of the chance they would have later to share their thoughts and feelings on the session (59), and to work out with students or reveal to them how "success" of the lesson is to be determined—an increase in the number of higher level questions asked by the class, for example.

Right from the start (3), the teacher makes it clear that today's session will be inquiry-oriented, and that he will serve as a guide to aid pupil cognitive growth (5, 16) and their use of effective processes (18)—he helps Maria see Gina's possible feelings of being cut off; (56—he models a paraphrase). He had, to be sure, established his role as guide by providing the original encounter (2).

With regard to helping students develop their inquiry skills, the teacher refrains from judging student response (24-26), but rather suggests an operation (24) and seems willing to allow students to proceed at their own individual paces for learning (31-33). Serving, perhaps deliberately, as a model for inquiry skills and processes as well as a guide, he uses a divergent-type questions (44), and he asks increasingly sophisticated questions (12 requires a simple "Yes, No"; 26 solicits active investigation; and 50 encourages the clear stating of a hypothesis). When the teacher responds to a student question, he does so directly (7) or he utilizes probe techniques (22, 54) to refer the concern back to the student for additional investigation and thinking. He would, we might guess, continue to use questions in later sessions to help students identify and examine their own processes of inquiry—the kinds and levels of questions they are using, or not using, for example. The teacher, at least at this stage, seems to be in charge of his own behavior of question-asking. In terms of "product" achievement, by the way, his maneuvers noting the product of student inquiry (50) and his overall use of questions assists students to move in their thinking from a sort of guessing status (6) into the generation (and testing) of reasonable and reasoned hypotheses (51-52; 66-67).

Although the whole atmosphere of the session seems open and conducive to inquiring— the lesson develops on student questions and responses, for instance—it also seems more teacher-centered than necessary. For example, a teacher using the discovery strategy need not initiate and/or respond to all questions as is the case here. If this element of teacher strategy were replaced (student questions could be "handed over" to other students by teacher nonverbal gestures and/or teacher silence, for example), students might be more likely, in the arena of student-student interaction, to examine and identify (with teacher help) their own processes and skills of inquiry. They might also develop more thorough support for their statements than is evident in the observed episode. Further, the teacher following this more nondirective approach could free himself to reward students for their creative hypotheses and applications of inquiry thinking. To illustrate, Maria's question, "Is your hand warm?" (23) could be followed with, "That sounds like you're on the track of a solid hypothesis, Maria—good, you are questioning logically!"

At the conclusion of the session, there is no "closure" in the sense of ending inquiry. Rather, the teacher pauses to focus student attention on the processes in inquiry with which they have been involved (59, 61) and then seems to encourage further investigation (67). It looks as if in the next lesson, students will continue to use and expand their inquiry skills with a teacher who not only serves as a guide but also as a model for their discovery learning experiences.

NOTES

1. N. L. Gage, "Teaching Methods," *Encyclopedia of Educational Research* (New York: Macmillan Co., 1969), p. 1456.

2. John P. DeCecce and William R. Crawford, *The Psychology of Learning and Instruction* (Englewood Cliffs, N. J.: Prentice-Hall, 1974), p. 357.

3. Robert F. Biehler, *Psychology Applied to Teaching* (Boston: Houghton Mifflin Co., 1971), pp. 231, 233.

4. N. L. Gage, *loc. cit.*

5. As quoted in Dwight W. Allen and Eli Seifman, *The Teacher's Handbook* (Glenview, Ill.: Scott, Foresman and Co., 1971), pp. 56-57. (Reprinted by permission.)

6. As quoted in Ben B. Strasser et. al., *Teaching Toward Inquiry* (Washington, D.C.: National Education Association, 1971), pp. 80-86. (Reprinted by permission.)

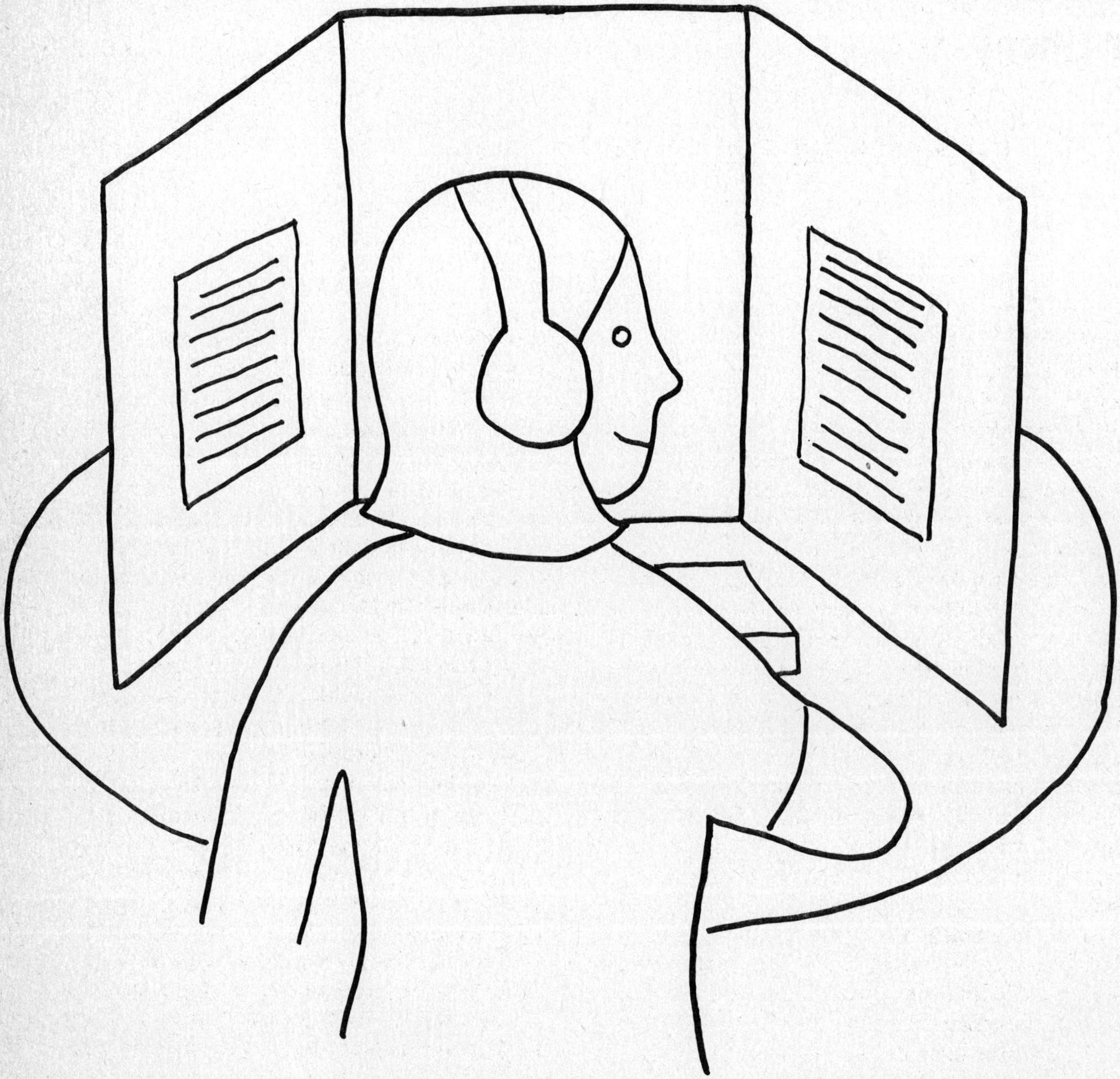

strategy 8

The Learning Center

BACKGROUND

Recognition of the differences among individuals as a reality of life goes back to the time of ancient Greece and such early teachers as Socrates and Plato. Philosophers and educators since that time have envisioned ways of providing for these individual differences through a variety of methods and organizational patterns.

The graded system, established in American schools in 1870, was an early attempt to limit the range of differences in order to provide more individualized instruction. It was not until years later that educators began to realize that—even when students are grouped in grades according to chronological age—many differences still exist among those within each grade, and providing for individual differences requires means for permitting each child to progress at the rate that is normal for him, whether that rate be rapid or slow.[1]

A more recent attempt at individualizing instruction is the strategy of the *learning center*, which is a loose term for an area in the classroom or some designated area in the school where there is a wide assortment of resources for learning, and where the emphasis is on making observable gains in learning and in improving the pupils' self-management of that learning.

Although learning centers in the above definition are viewed as "where" one teaches rather than "how" one teaches, we believe the teacher behaviors associated with the planning and development of learning centers meet the requirements of the definition of an instructional strategy, which we indicated in the introduction was used as a criterion for selecting the twelve strategies included in this book.

Although the learning center strategy appears to be a natural outgrowth of the continued search for ways to individualize instruction, which has been supported through research and practice, the search has been intensified by the recent social and economic pressures on public school educators to be more accountable for their work with students. (Performance-based instruction, an outcome of these pressures, is discussed in more detail in Strategy 11, the section describing learning activity packages.)

The most influential recent research supporting a more individualized approach to instruction is that of Jean Piaget, the noted Swiss child psychologist. His description of how children acquire an understanding of number and space and how they develop cognitive processes has been considered important for a number of years in Europe and England, and his writings are now discussed and studied in the United States. The basic findings from his research are that children learn in a series of developmental stages, in repeated encounters with concrete experiences, and in exchanges of differing points of view. Acting upon Piaget's research would require a classroom environment for elementary children that allows them to explore with concrete materials and to interact with each other as well as with the teacher. Piaget's research has greatly influenced practice in England, where objects and materials have been organized into learning areas that promote self-direction and a more informal learning environment.[2]

Although many American schools have moved totally into the open environment practiced in England, others have begun to use the learning center strategy as an initial step toward the more informal learning setting that is encouraged by current educational thought. The move toward a greater use of learning centers is taking place at both the elementary and secondary levels, as the two classroom examples included in this section reveal. In many cases, learning centers are being used in traditional classroom settings through a creative use of space and equipment. Although learning centers can also be effectively used in open-space learning settings, an open-space school is not a requisite for the use of the learning center strategy. Neither should learning centers be thought of as being used by only one student. Individualization of instruction can also take place in small groups, and centers can be planned for groups of students to use at the same time as well.

The greater use of the learning center strategy has revealed much creativity on the part of teachers and their students in developing areas of learning in the traditional classroom. As Imogene Forte and Joy Mackenzie describe in their practical book *Nooks, Crannies and Corners*, "bookcases, large cardboard boxes, easels, walls, window sills, window shades, doors, closets, backs and sides of desks, pianos, and lockers, hallways, the playground, and even the ceiling may be utilized as space for learning."[3]

In other school situations, total classrooms have been set aside as "math centers," "science centers," etc., with individualized activities available for the students. Whether in a regular classroom or a designated center within the schools, there is frequent use of various media and of the abundant commercial material currently available.

Most educators who write about the learning center strategy urge teachers to move gradually into the use of the strategy after carefully reviewing the purposes and suggested procedures for this approach. Fortunately, it is a strategy that can begin and continue with one step at a time. Many teachers are taking that first step and finding it a very worthwhile approach to individualizing instruction.

COMPETENCY WORKSHEET FOR PLANNING AND OBSERVING

Checkpoints   **Observer Notes**

When using the learning center strategy, the teacher is usually observed performing the following behaviors:

_____ Organizing the curriculum for partial or total conversion to learning centers.

_____ Identifying the objectives to be accomplished through the learning centers, with consideration given to student needs, interests, and abilities.

_____ Selecting an appropriate format for the center; e.g., three-paneled carrel, bulletin board, poster, etc.

_____ Selecting materials needed to accomplish the objectives, as well as procedures for evaluating each student's attainment of these objectives, using multi-media equipment whenever possible; e.g., tape recorders, film-strip projectors.

_____ Devising an eye-catching, thought-provoking title that will motivate the student to use the center.

_____ Preparing directions for the center that are easy to locate, understand, and follow.

_____ Developing a pre-assessment activity, if the teacher believes one is needed.

_____ Developing guiding questions for inclusion at the centers; these must be open-ended and varied, so that each student can achieve success at his/her ability level; e.g., "List as many as you can of _____ ."

_____ Providing optional activities, so that students will have several ways of accomplishing similar objectives.

_____ Determining how students will maintain a record of their activities at the center; e.g., a checklist may be kept at each center with all students' names listed. When a student successfully completes the center, he checks his name in the appropriate space.

_____ Orienting students to the use of the centers; e.g., information is given on traffic patterns, freedom of movement among centers, proper use of materials, overall goals and purposes, recommended time for completing centers, and initial assignments.

_____ Encouraging students, in groups or as individuals, to express their ideas, to create their own solutions, and/or to engage in exchange of ideas and justification of their responses; e.g., students may want to discuss what they are learning at the centers with the teacher as well as with other students.

_____ Using other students and parents as aides in accomplishing the objectives of the centers.

_____ Conducting regular, planned conferences with the students to review their progress and evaluate how well they have accomplished the objectives of the center.

_____ Serving as a resource to the students as they need assistance in completing the centers.

_____ Replacing centers that have been used, as determined by student feedback and need; e.g., the teacher may develop and try out a new center or bring out of storage one that seems appropriate.

SOME ADVANTAGES

The following are often mentioned as some of the advantages of the learning center strategy:

- It is appropriate for use in settings that range from self-contained elementary and secondary classrooms to modern, open schools.
- It can be used to develop understandings, skills, and attitudes.
- It allows students to proceed at their own pace and ability level; e.g., centers can promote higher levels of intellectual activity through open-ended questions.
- The strategy promotes continuous review of student progress, through self-evaluation and regular conferences with the teacher.
- It can provide for the different learning styles of students; e.g., use of multi-media materials is encouraged.
- It provides opportunities to develop a more varied curriculum, by taking advantage of the immediate interests and needs of students. This may be more characteristic of the use of centers in elementary schools, however, where the curriculum sometimes is more flexible.

- It frees teachers to serve more as learning facilitators, observers, and consultants to individual students. This strategy can more fully utilize the total professional background of the teacher.

SOME DISADVANTAGES
The following are often mentioned as some of the disadvantages of the learning center strategy:

- It encourages an active learning environment that may be unfamiliar and uncomfortable for some students and teachers as well as for administrators and parents who have not been introduced to the values of this approach. The untraditional room arrangement may be annoying to some school custodians.

- It requires a greater amount of initial preparation time for teachers than do more traditional methods.

- It necessitates a change to a teaching style that may not be the best one for all teachers.

- It requires systematic record-keeping for maximum effectiveness, which might be viewed by some teachers as an inappropriate use of their time.

- The strategy stresses independent work skills, and thus it may be difficult for students who have not yet developed such skills.

- It necessitates the recruitment of teacher aides, if centers are used as the primary method of instruction. Volunteer aides are not always readily available or effective, and the budget may not provide for paid instructional aides.

CLASSROOM EXAMPLE (ELEMENTARY)
In this middle-elementary classroom, the teacher has moved partially into the use of learning centers as a method for individualizing instruction. She has selected one center that focuses on a specific skill, another that presents information, and a third that is just for fun. The children who have completed their assigned work are given the opportunity to use the centers, which are placed in three separate areas of the classroom.

One child is using the skill center, which focuses on hand-writing. The teacher's objective for this center is to improve letter formation and spelling. She has included in the center handwriting samples to copy, paper, and pencils. Her directions are written on a piece of cardboard that has been attached to the wall in front of a large table. The directions read: (1) pick a paper, (2) write what's on the paper, (3) do six different papers to finish the center. The student is asked to evaluate his skill by comparing his writing with the sample and to check with the letter formation chart. There is a pocket on the chart for completed papers.

At the information center, another child is reading the directions that are listed on a display made out of two heavy pieces of cardboard taped together and placed on a low bookshelf. The title is "Let's Learn About Indians." The teacher's objective at this center is to supplement with related material the information in the unit study of Indians presented in the textbook. At the center are programed materials (text and records), record player, and earphones. The directions are: (1) sit down, (2) put on earphones, (3) turn to page ____ , (4) put on record number ____ , (5) now look and listen. The evaluation suggestions listed at the center indicate that evaluation will take place during teacher/class discussions of material covered within the center and at teacher/student conferences in which students retell the story, using the pictures in the text.

In the fun center, art materials are on the window sill in a cardboard box for the children to use in any way they may like. The box contains assorted paper, paste, scissors, and other odds and ends the teacher has collected. No specific behavioral objective is identified; the objective is for the students to have a pleasurable experience with the art materials. The sign over the center says: TRY IT!

Analysis/Comment (Elementary)
The teacher in this example was situated in a traditional, self-contained classroom. She had obviously decided to move slowly with this new strategy and to try out a variety of centers for different areas of the curriculum—language arts, social studies, and art; the centers had been

planned for those children who had completed their assigned work rather than on a careful diagnosis of individual needs. Most likely, however, the teacher saw her initial efforts to use the learning center strategy as a learning experience for herself as well as for the children, and she had selected activities with which the children could be successful as they experienced a new way of learning. Hopefully, she would eventually allow all of the children to have an opportunity to try the centers; her current procedures may prevent the very slow child from ever doing so.

The teacher made an interesting use of space in setting up the centers in the classroom. One center was a poster attached to a wall, with a table for writing in front of it; a second was two pieces of cardboard taped together and placed on a low bookshelf containing the media equipment and books needed; and the art center was a cardboard box on the window sill. The teacher had obviously been successful in making these centers attractive to the students, because they were being used in this classroom. If centers are new to a group, however, the children are usually eager to try them, even if the centers are not particularly colorful or do not have eye-catching titles.

The children did not appear to have any difficulty with the directions, which were simple and direct. Most likely the teacher had talked with them prior to this observation, explaining the purpose of each center, how to use them, the times when they would be available, and opportunities for the children to share with her their opinions of the centers.

There was nothing in the example to indicate how the teacher would keep a record of who used the centers and what they accomplished. Most likely she would have seen the need for this as she and the children gained more experience in using the centers.

The teacher probably planned to divide her time between the children at the centers and those completing their assigned work at their desks. During the period described, she was working only with those still doing their desk work. As others moved to the centers, she would probably have tried to provide additional assistance for them.

The main point to be made from this example is that the teacher was looking for new ways to work with the children and believed the learning center strategy to be one that might work in her classroom. She was giving it a try. She and the children were learning how to use a new way of teaching and learning that has much potential for individualizing instruction.

CLASSROOM EXAMPLE (SECONDARY)

The senior high school teacher in this example felt a need to help her students reconsider certain of the process skills they had studied earlier in the year. She considered the processes of "observing," "problem solving," "elaborating," "deciding," and "perceiving" as being the most important for students to work on at this point in the school year. To implement her objective, she chose the learning center strategy and, with the aid of selected students, she developed a number of process-oriented learning centers. These were set up in various areas of the classroom, and three class periods were planned for students to engage themselves with the centers. The teacher made it clear that each student should visit all five centers during the three periods provided and that she would be consistently available for help.

Each of the five centers—one for each process—was organized essentially in the following manner. A card posted at the center indicated its name; for example, "Problem Solving." Directions on mimeographed handouts were placed conspicuously at the center, so that more than one student at a time could use the center and all would find it easy to read the directions. The directions at the center on problem solving asked each student choosing this center to pick one or two other persons with whom to work. Then the student was to pick a card from the large envelope and read the problem on the card aloud to his group. Following this, he was to "brainstorm" with the group regarding possible ways of dealing with the problem and, perhaps, even ways of solving it. The students were asked to keep a written record of the results of their brainstorming.

The student who drew the card was then to turn the card over and allow the group to compare responses on the card with those generated in their group brainstorm. None of the alternatives on the card was indicated as a "right" or "wrong" response. Finally, the student drawing the original card was asked to lead a group debriefing discussion on the following questions:

> What characterized our approach to the problem?
>
> What models for problem solving did we generate?
>
> What do these models have in common?
>
> What was the most creative idea the group had?

Answers to these questions, along with the number of the problem card, the name of the station, and the name of the student originating the action at the center, were to be turned in to the teacher for appropriate feedback and record-keeping.

The teacher reviewed the general directions, overall goal and purposes of the centers, and encouraged students to begin.

Analysis/Comment (Secondary)
A commitment to the learning center strategy has been made by this teacher—and it seems an appropriate decision. However, she might do well in the future to corroborate her estimate of pupil need with the students and to tie in her plans to *student* need as well as to her own by checking with the students. She has obviously chosen in advance the type of learning centers to be used, process centers, and she has wisely enlisted the help of students in developing them. Here is a source of energy and creativity too often overlooked in center construction. Student involvement at this point helps them feel a part of what should be a continuing learning encounter in the classroom, and it also facilitates their learning, informally, the very processes the centers being planned are designed to teach. Students can, for instance, learn "problem solving" by facing the problem of building a center on problem solving! Selected students might even be used during the three days to help other students. They could serve as assistant teachers, depending on their own competency levels with the processes.

From lack of evidence to the contrary, it might be assumed that the teacher seemed to be confident of student maturity to work effectively in a center environment; further, she seemed to have a good plan for arranging the room to accommodate the centers. Use of the checklist during the actual teaching would provide more objective data on which to base or retract these assumptions.

Although the teacher reviewed the purposes, in general, of the center approach in the students' present curriculum—one of them seems to be to help students gain more competence in five basic processes—the purposes could be made clearer. Maybe they are, to the teacher. The specific objectives might also be spelled out, to benefit both the teacher and the students. Making it clear what the centers are supposed to do, and why, could be done through class interaction or through information at the centers themselves. The learning center described seems to come up a bit short in terms of any precise way a student should be different after having "done" the center. The teacher's behavior as exhibited in the Classroom Example could be interpreted to mean that she has not clearly defined the behavioral changes that she would like to have take place through the students' use of the centers.

Center directions are clear and accessible. More "excitement" could be put into the titles, perhaps, and multi-media aids could be built into the center experiences when the centers are rerun. The process orientation of the centers would tend to allow students to function at their own ability levels; in addition, the teacher has indicated her availability to supervise, in case some of the students have difficulty with what is asked either by the center directions or by another student. Note that the teacher has planned for the record keeping, which is another characteristic of the well-performed learning center strategy. She will ask students to turn in a series of written answers on open ended questions with appropriate identification. Moreover, she has committed herself to providing students with feedback on their thinking and learning as revealed by these answers. Through her comments, student learnings about the processes of problem solving can be reinforced, and through their comments, the teacher can determine where students "are" in relation to her goals for them.

In conclusion, the teacher might want to schedule regular conferences with students to talk with them about their progress. The papers turned in could serve as evidence of student work that she could have with her for the conferences. She might want to replace some of the centers with fresh ones, if students need new ones now or later to help them reach the objectives selected. With her evident interest in the center strategy, she could return to the strategy again for the same purposes or for others. She seems to have an appreciation and a working understanding of how the strategy can be used to help students express ideas, create solutions, and engage in exchange of ideas and justification regarding their responses.

NOTES

1. *Individualization in Schools: The Challenge and the Options* (Washington, D.C.: National School Public Relations Association, 1971), pp. 1-3.

2. John Blackie, *Inside the Primary School* (New York: Schocken Books, 1971), pp. 27-34.

3. Imogene Forte and Joy Mackenzie, *Nooks, Crannies and Corners: Learning Centers for Creative Classrooms* (Nashville, Tenn.: Incentive Publications, 1972) p. 106.

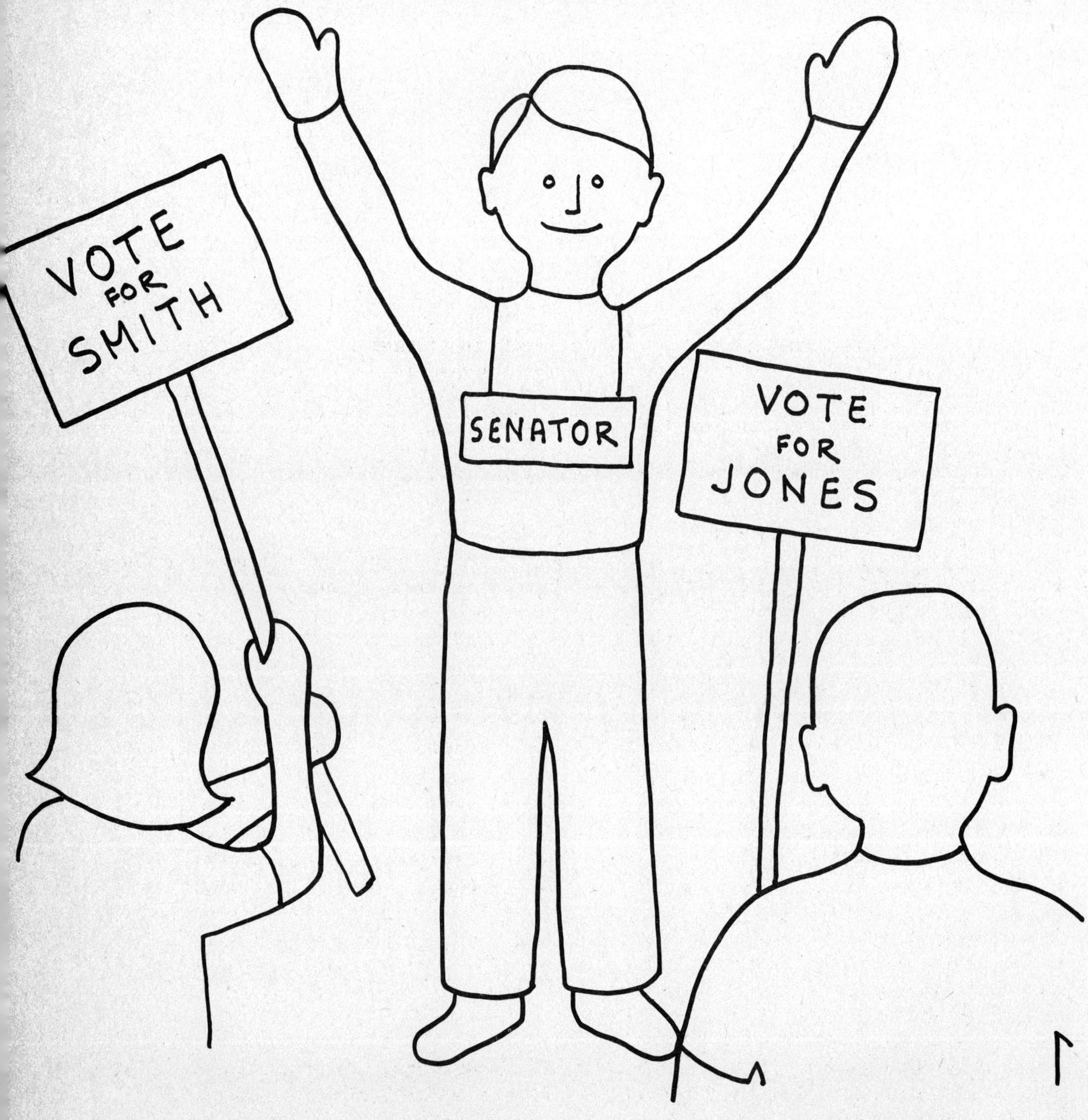
VOTE FOR SMITH
SENATOR
VOTE FOR JONES

strategy 9

Simulation

BACKGROUND

Have you ever been in a classroom where you were asked to pretend to be someone else, for the purpose of learning more about how other people feel and act? Have you ever played a game in which you had the opportunity to be someone other than yourself—and in the process of having a good time you got a better idea of what that other person might be like? If your answer is yes to one or both of these questions, then you have been involved in the strategy known as *simulation*.

In the most general terms, simulation is defined by Paul A. Twelker [1] as obtaining the essence of something but without all aspects of reality. Its purpose for elementary and secondary students is to provide a wide assortment of adult-type encounters, without fear of serious reprisal from wrong actions or judgments. According to Ronald T. Hyman these encounters can come through role playing, sociodramas, or simulation games. [2]

Role playing is the acting out of roles decided upon in advance, for such purposes as re-creating historical scenes of the past, possible events of the future, significant current events, or imaginary situations at any place or time. The student "crawls into the skin" of another individual, and by recreating the person's actions gains a better understanding of the person and the motivations that prompted his behavior.

Sociodrama is a group problem-solving enactment that focuses on a problem involving human relations. The problem might be related to students' work together in the school, family, or community. Sociodramas offer students the opportunity to explore alternative solutions to problems of concern to the group.

Simulation games are those in which the students assume specific roles as decision-makers, act as if they were actually involved in the situation, and compete for certain objectives according to specified rules. One of the best known board games in our present society is "Monopoly," a simulation of the real estate business. An analysis of the literature reveals, however, that even after a decade of development and implementation, little is known about the impact of simulation games on the cognitive and affective development of the student. [3]

The development of the simulation strategy can be traced back to at least three ancestors: simulator trainers, games, and role playing. Simulator trainers were developed by the aerospace industry for the purpose of teaching airplane pilots, and later astronauts, to manipulate a simulated environment and thus, by implication, the real one. Games have been a part of most cultures and are usually looked upon as pleasant and stimulating. They have usually been thought of as competitive encounters among individuals, involving some degree of skill and/or luck. Role playing is another natural part of a young human being's play activities. Children enjoy acting out the various roles that they see others playing or that appear in their favorite stories.[4]

From these rather different heritages have evolved the educational innovations that are now grouped under the heading of simulation.

COMPETENCY WORKSHEET FOR PLANNING AND OBSERVING

Checkpoints

Observer Notes

When using the simulation strategy, the teacher is usually observed performing the following behaviors:

_____ Selecting an appropriate situation, problem, or game that helps the group move toward stated instructional objectives, through role playing, sociodrama, or simulation.

_____ Organizing for the activity so that the roles and responsibilities are clear, and materials, time, and space are adequate.

_____ Preparing directions that are clear to the students involved and that clarify how this activity will assist in accomplishing identified objectives.

_____ Stating these directions clearly to students.

_____ Answering questions related to the activity.

_____ Selecting students for this activity who represent the varying abilities in the classroom or who would most profit from the use of this strategy.

_____ Assisting the students involved, during their initial planning session.

_____ Supervising the activity to ensure that roles and responsibilities are being carried out according to the agreed-on rules or guidelines.

_____ Offering suggestions for improving the activity while it is in progress.

_____ Conducting an evaluation of the activity that focuses on the contributions of the activity to improving students' understanding of the objectives to be reached, as well as on improvements for the next simulation activity.

SOME ADVANTAGES
The following are often mentioned as some of the advantages of the simulation strategy:

- Simulation activities are fun. Students are naturally motivated to participate.

- The strategy encourages teachers to develop their own simulation activities with or without the assistance of the students.

- It allows for types of experimentation that cannot take place in the real environment.

- It reduces the level of abstraction, even when the concept being explored is abstract, because the student is directly involved in the activity.

- The strategy does not necessarily require the student to have sophisticated communication skills. In many cases, the student may need only simple directions.

- It requires the type of interaction among students that can be conducive to class unity.

- The strategy often elicits a positive response from students who are slow, disadvantaged, or unmotivated.

- Many simulation activities promote and reward critical thinking, because they involve analyzing possible moves and probable consequences of these moves.

- The strategy allows teachers to work with a wide range of student capabilities at the same time.

SOME DISADVANTAGES
The following are often mentioned as some of the disadvantages of the simulation strategy:

- Its effectiveness in improving learning has not been established by current research.

- It can be expensive since most commercial simulation games are costly causing opponents to ask whether a mere increase in motivation is sufficient to justify extensive use of this strategy.

- It prompts many people to question the validity of simulation techniques which sometimes screen out important elements; e.g., the driver education simulator may not include traffic, noise, and the need for considering others on the road.

- The strategy requires flexible groupings of students, as well as actual fluidity of movement within the classroom and building.

- This strategy requires much imagination on the part of the teacher and students.

- Simulation activities promote a more informal relationship between the teacher and the students. This may make some teachers and pupils uncomfortable because it is a change from the normal teacher-pupil relationship that prevails in many schools.

- The strategy sometimes invites parental criticism since its activities involve play.

CLASSROOM EXAMPLE (ELEMENTARY)

Although this elementary teacher has organized his classroom activities so that much time is spent in small-group work and independent study, he selected on the day before this observation to use a simulation strategy for a large-group activity in social studies. His fifth-grade class is studying the effects of mass production on employees and the products they produce.

On the first day of the simulated activity, each student was asked to play the role of an employee in the "Original Hand-Colored Art Factory." Every student was given three crayons (black, pink, and blue) and a mimeographed picture of George Washington. The teacher, playing the role of the factory manager, asked the workers to color their pictures using their three crayons and to do the very best that they possibly could. The manager explained that the employees could spend as long as they liked and could even take the pictures home to finish if they so desired.

On the day of the observation, the children have displayed their work on a bulletin board, leaving a space beside each picture for another picture which is to be completed by methods characteristic of mass production. After they had put up their pictures, the children were asked by the factory manager to clear their desks. He then gave each of them another picture of George Washington that had been prepared in sections, similar to the popular paint-by-number pictures that are found in hobby shops.

There were 25 numbered sections on each picture, enough for each child to have one space to color. The teacher assigned each child the number of the space he or she was to color and gave each child either a black, pink, or blue crayon. The teacher explained that when he rang the bell, each worker should color his assigned space and then should pass the paper on to the worker to his right when the bell was rung again.

The teacher rang the bell and waited five minutes. (He looked around the room to be certain that all children had completed the coloring of their assigned spaces before ringing the bell again.) Each time, however, he gave the factory workers a little less time to do their work. When workers had completed coloring their parts on each of the 25 pictures, they were given a snack break. When all pictures had been completed, each child was given one to display on the bulletin board beside the picture he had colored completely by himself the day before.

Still playing the role of employees in the "Original Hand-Colored Art Factory," the children were called to a meeting with the factory manager to discuss the two methods used in creating hand-colored pictures of George Washington and the effect of these methods on their work. The manager listed the advantages and disadvantages identified by his employees in producing the paintings and then commented on them from his point of view as a manager and part-owner of the factory.

When the simulation was over, the teacher and the children talked about what they had learned from it.

Analysis/Comment (Elementary)

Using the role-playing approach to simulation, this young teacher followed most of the points included on the competency worksheet. The situation selected was most appropriate for role playing. The children were not only given the opportunity to pretend to be workers in a factory, they became workers through the production of a specific project. They could thus comment on the actual effect that the two approaches used by the manager had on them.

The teacher also extended the strategy over two periods rather than attempting to complete it on the first day. This gave the children an opportunity to become more intensely involved in the simulation, to share ideas with one another, and to talk with their families about their feelings as workers in the "Original Hand-Colored Art Factory."

The children appeared to understand their roles well, and hopefully the objectives of the simulation were clear to them. Because the classroom observation did not reveal how the teacher had initiated this simulation activity, we can only assume that the students saw value in what they were doing and realized that their teacher was helping them move toward a better understanding of mass production as it is sometimes practiced within our society.

Another advantage of this simulation example is that everyone in the class, including the teacher, was actively involved. The teacher did not have to be concerned with the checkpoint indicating that teachers usually select students who represent the varying abilities in the classroom, because he made this simulation a class activity with a part for everyone.

The teacher obviously enjoyed and felt comfortable with the use of this strategy. He had carefully thought through various details such as the two types of pictures needed, the limited range of crayon colors, and the use of the bulletin board for displaying the products of the children. Although he was working within a typical elementary classroom, he had made effective use of the limited space.

The classroom example closes with the evaluation by the students. The students appeared most excited about this approach to teaching and believed that they had a better understanding of mass production because of it. Although the learnings each child gained from this experience were intensely personal, most of them seemed to believe the activity was worthwhile because it had brought them closer to an aspect of their society about which they knew very little. The simulation strategy as effectively used by their teacher had provided a creative environment in which this realization could take place.

CLASSROOM EXAMPLE (SECONDARY)

For this classroom example, we observe the fourth day of a simulation experience in a secondary social studies classroom. The class is working with COPE,[4] a simulation of adapting to change and anticipating the future. From a quick review of a *Student Guide* to the simulation loaned by a member of the class, we get the same overview of the game that students have and also note a series of broad "thought questions" that the students are to keep before them as they work through the simulation. The setting of the simulation is Technopolis, a future city into which students have been born and in which they will experience life during five different time periods. A more detailed history of Technopolis, from 1970-1990, is available on a handout that students have in their notebooks.

On this particular day, students are living in Time Period 2. A complex computer called COMCON is available to help with information and material problems. The students had received a typical print-out from the computer which had asked citizens to provide human input for problems that must be solved. They are working on particular tasks in the two loosely organized groups that are recommended by the game plan at this point. A Community Council to which each group will send three representatives will be meeting in a "fishbowl" discussion in about 30 minutes. All the students seem to be involved. The members of one group call themselves "Humanists"—citizens who think and plan for the future in strictly human terms. Other students have organized themselves during previous sessions into the "Engineers" group, which thinks and plans for the future in scientific and technological terms.

The Humanist group is doing a "think-tank" project tied in to print-out information on the greater percentage of time spent by humans on leisure activities and hobbies than on work efforts. This group is in the process of developing some guidelines not only for justifying but also for recommending the desirablility of "becoming a person" through expanding one's interests and abilities. They are *not* in favor of recent and increasingly strong emphases for the society to produce eating and resting and hobby systems that do not interfere with efficiency and productivity. "Old" books of the 1970s (for example, *What Do You Say After You Say Hello?* and *Go Ask Alice*) are a prime resource for the Humanist group. Each book read is "punched into" a data bank card with author, title, nature of contents, topics covered, important ideas, and reviewer's opinion. The cards are maintained in a central file for possible feeding in to COMCON.

The Engineers, meanwhile, are doing what the game identifies as a productive task. They are solving a game problem relating to the Toffler Foundation. It has been noted by COMCON that this futurists' organization, popular in the early 1980's, has been bothered by a lack of space in recent years. The Engineers have undertaken a study of nonverbal behavior, especially in relation to the dimension of space and how it communicates, in an effort to cope with the problem. Copies of *The Silent Language* and *The Hidden Dimension*, both by Edward T. Hall, are available in the room. The Engineers are also in the process of redesigning the building in line with their findings. (An expected grant should make reconstruction possible.) Actual blueprints are being drawn up as is a set of recommendations, with supporting evidence and rationale, for making the present situation more "effective" and "productive." Their past preferences, as revealed by the supervising teacher, indicate that the Engineers tend to like these last two terms. But one girl, evidently not so sure anymore—or perhaps merely curious—goes to work with the Humanist group, as we watch.

For each task, students can claim a predetermined number of Creative Work Units (CWU's), representing wealth in the simulation (and a substantial portion of their grade for this unit). Class members in the Engineers group, for instance, can claim from 100 to 150 CWU's, depending on how they adhere to such criteria as following directions, completing the task, and devising creative approaches or solutions. An individual CWU Data Card is maintained by each student; he records the date, the number of CWU's gained or lost, and the new balance. A place for "terminal balance" will contain his number of CWU's at the end of the simulation unit. The teacher keeps a master record.

The Council meeting begins. It uses the "open chair" technique, permitting anyone from the outside ring of the fishbowl to enter, make a point, and return. Involved in the meeting are roles played in relation to the jobs of the simulation. But there is also a move into real-life analysis, keyed, actually, to several of the thought questions presented at the start of the unit: "Can we cause the kind of future we prefer to have?" and "Can we adapt quickly enough to keep up with the pace of change?" As the period draws to a close, on the recommendation of the teacher the Council decides to consider further discussion on group findings and to entertain additional general discussion after students get into the creative and productive tasks of the next Creative Production Module, some ten more years in the future.

At this point, the period ends.

Analysis /Comment (Secondary)

Immediately striking in this use of the simulation strategy is the low profile of the teacher. He serves as a supervisor who helps students adhere to presumably agreed-on rules or guidelines. (He avoids "blocking" when a student chooses to leave one group for another, for instance.) He also seems to make explanations and suggestions when needed—such as recommending moving into the third time period of the game. Overall, it is evident that the teacher is maintaining professional responsibility for what is going on in the classroom but is doing so without being the consistent center of attraction. This, we would suggest, is a good thing! One supporting indication of his accepting underlying responsibility is the use of thought questions that suggest a clear purpose in the teacher's mind for using this simulation game in the first place. The questions seem to embody at least two instructional goals. That is, the ones discussed in the Council meeting could lead students into an analysis of their value systems and an inventory of their personal capabilities for coping with change. Notice that the teacher also stops the game at a high point (coinciding with the end of the period), a move that facilitates a carry-over of pupil interest.

Through the simulation, the students are working toward the goals in the framework of an instructional strategy that gives them freedom to try their own ideas and to increase their own abilities to accept responsibility and solve problems. The simulation and its tasks, both individual (e.g., prepare and present your own ideas about what future life styles should be) and group (e.g., develop a set of blueprints and a group working style that is efficient and productive), merely gets them started.

A few observations that might need to be called to the attention of this teacher have to do with his inclusion of all students in the simulation. Perhaps some students would be helped more by working by themselves—at least for a while—rather than by being members of a group. Making written notes would also be worthy of consideration. Too many things happen in simulation for a teacher to rely, at least consistently, on mental notes. Written notes would help in the evaluation that is part of simulation. True, the students did a kind of evaluation in their Council meeting, and the CWU's they obtain act as an evaluative device. But the teacher's broader, and probably deeper, appreciation for what went on could provide another dimension. It could refocus student attention on what objectives they are working on, why and how they are achieving these now, and how they might work on them in the rest of the simulation exercise. Use of the checkpoints in the actual teaching situation would tend to make subsequent self-analysis by the teacher less subjective. For example, he could remember to check for himself: Is this game particularly appropriate for these students? Were the goals clearly stated in advance? Was the game shown to connect to the goals? Were students helped to get started? However, giving him the benefit of doubt along the line, perhaps we can also assume the other checklist items are being observed. The evident work emphasis of the students suggests that clear directions, work space, and the like are appropriately provided. In all, it seems fair to say the simulation strategy is used here rather accurately—according to the checkpoints—and well.

NOTES

1. Paul A. Twelker, "A Basic Reference Shelf on Simulation and Gaming," David W. Zuckerman and Robert E. Horn, *The Guide to Simulation Games for Education and Training* (Cambridge, Mass.: Information Resource), p. 313.

2. Ronald T. Hyman, *Ways of Teaching* (New York: J. P. Lippincott, 1970), pp. 167-213.

3. Everett T. Keach, Jr., and David A. Pierfy, "Simulation Games: Facts and Fancies," *Childhood Education* 50 (March 1974), pp. 307-310.

4. Paul A. Twelker, op. cit., p. 313.

5. Adapted from *COPE: A Simulation of Adapting to Change and Anticipating the Future* by Jerry K. Ward (Lakeside, Calif. Interact Co.,) 1972.

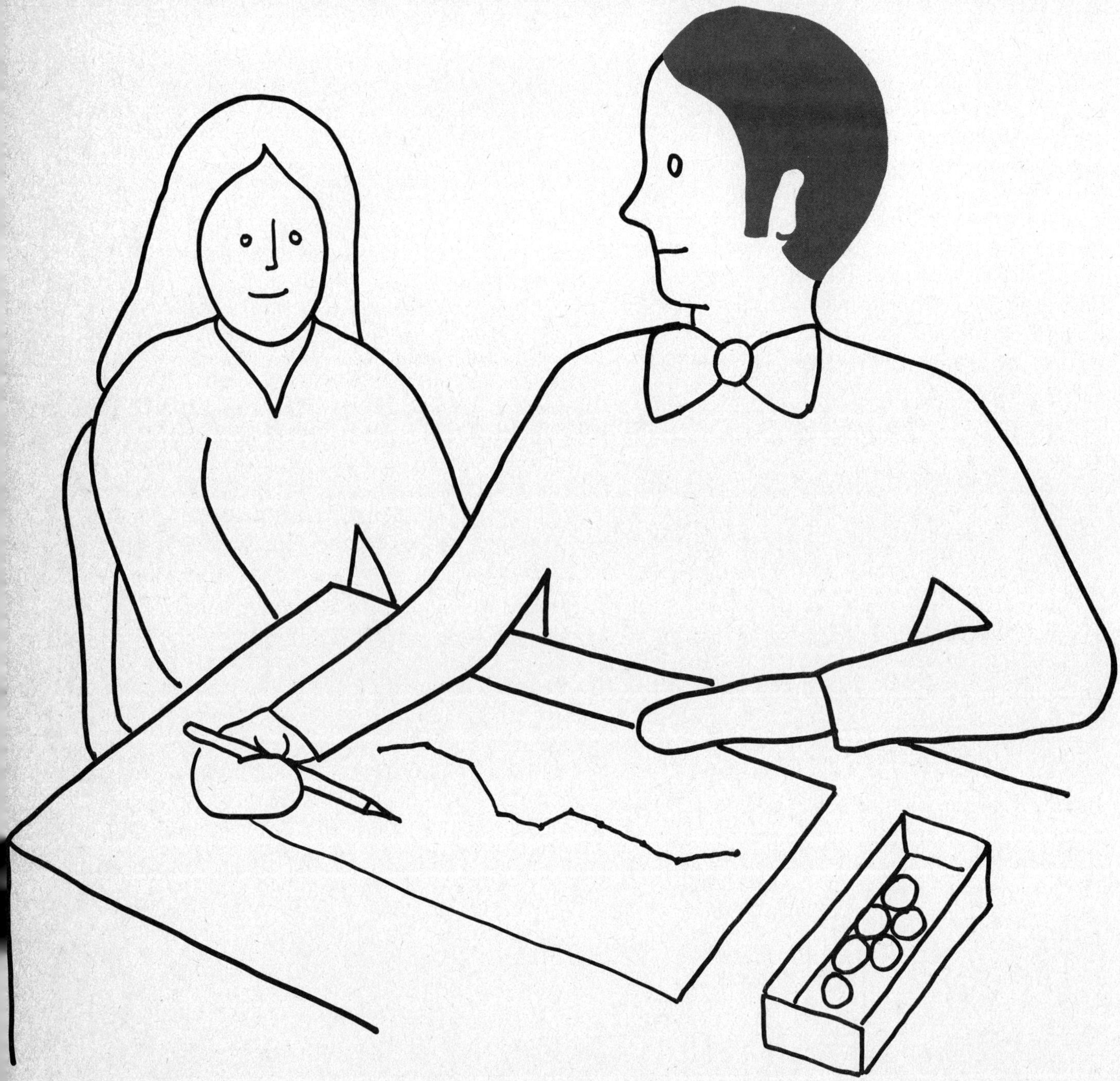

strategy 10

Behavior Modification

BACKGROUND

One of the more recent and more controversial methods currently being used in both elementary and secondary classrooms is behavior modification. The term itself suggests a controlled environment in which children are being manipulated by insensitive teachers who have rigid, preconceived behavioral goals. The fact that the method has emerged from the studies of behavioral scientists such as B.F. Skinner has probably contributed to this clinical image, but many educators who are adapting the theories of the behaviorists to classroom settings view behavior modification as a new name for what some teachers have been doing throughout the years.

Madsen and Madsen, for example, write that behavior modification, when stripped to basics, "means changing behavior by rewarding the kind you want to encourage and ignoring or disapproving the kind you want to discourage." Many teachers use this method without thinking of it as a specific strategy for teaching. For them, it has become a natural way to handle large groups of learners.[1]

For the behavioral scientists, however, behavior modification represents a practical application of a major set of learning theories, which views learning as a conditioning process by which a person acquires a new response. Often referred to as *stimulus-response conditioning*, this theory of learning was developed by Edward Thorndike (1913) to explain how animals and human beings learn to make particular responses to particular stimuli in their environments. According to this theory, "two conditions provide for the gradual 'stamping in' of stimulus-response connections: The stimulus and the response must occur together, and the response must be followed by a satisfier, or reward."[2]

For example, Thorndike placed a hungry cat in a cage and a piece of fish outside. To obtain the fish, the cat had to pull a string that opened the cage door. Through trial and error, the cat gradually learned to pull the string that allowed it to escape from the cage and devour the fish. In this simple experiment, the key stimulus was the string that opened the cage, the key response was pulling the string, and the satisfier was the fish.[3] B.F. Skinner, a modern behavioral scientist, has continued experiments that extend Thorndike's earlier studies; Skinner has introduced programed learning materials and behavior modification techniques based on his principles of *operant conditioning*.

How widespread is the use of behavior modification in our schools? A precise answer to that question is quite difficult. If one thinks of behavior modification as the use of a teacher's normal system of rewards and punishments and disapprovals, then it can be found in most classrooms. If, however, one views it as a carefully planned program designed to lead the students to a predetermined goal through the use of rewards, the answer is less clear.

A recent survey completed at Northern Illinois University, involving 406 educators attending the 1973 summer session, revealed that most of the educators in the survey were familiar with the techniques used by professionals in behavior modification. This knowledge had been acquired primarily through college classwork, and to some extent it had been integrated into the respondents' teaching repertoires. Most of the educators questioned in this survey believed that it would be valuable to be trained in the use of behavior modification techniques in order to improve student/teacher interaction. They also regarded behavioral management as ethical; many saw it as effective in group control and applicable to education under present conditions. This sampling gives some idea of the use of and attitudes toward behavior modification.[4]

How effective is the method, once it has been incorporated into the teacher's repertoire? A body of research exploring the use of behavior modification to influence student performance is accumulating. Because of the diverse nature of the young people involved in this research and the specific aspects of the strategy being explored, generalizations about the strategy are reluctantly made. One of the most recent and comprehensive summaries of research, however, has been used in the Analysis/Comment section for the elementary example, where specific types of behavior modification incentives are discussed. Hopefully, readers seeking additional research evidence will read this research review in its entirety.[5]

As a strategy for helping to change all types of behaviors of all children, behavior modification requires a very thoughtful analysis by every educator—experienced and inexperienced. The material that follows provides a slightly different approach than those used in the other strategies, because behavior modification may be less familiar than are some of the others.

The competency worksheet represents a systematic approach to establishing a master plan for an individual student. The examples at each checkpoint illustrate how one student might move through each phase as described by Madsen and Madsen.[6]

The elementary classroom example that is included in this section is a collection of twelve vignettes that might be observed during a tour of an elementary school, rather than a look at one group of children or one child. An attempt is made to show the variety of ways in which behavior modification is used within many elementary schools.

The secondary example is a description of how one of the authors has used the behavior modification strategy in working with future teachers.

COMPETENCY WORKSHEET FOR PLANNING AND OBSERVING

Checkpoints   **Observer Notes**

When using the behavior modification strategy, the teacher is usually observed performing the following behaviors:

_____ Pinpointing the specific behavior that might be changed; e.g., a student wastes time in class when given the opportunity to complete work assigned by the teacher. As a result, he is falling farther and farther behind, although his test scores indicate he has the ability to do the work.

_____ Observing the student closely to determine how often he or she is demonstrating the behavior that is to be changed; e.g., the teacher keeps a record of when and how often the student postpones doing assigned work. Does this occur daily or only on certain days of the week? Is the behavior becoming more frequent or less frequent?

_____ Discussing with the student the behavior that is preventing him from succeeding with school work; e.g., in a conference setting, the teacher may share with the student the results of her observations, review the student's progress, and indicate a desire to help the student change his behavior so that he will be more successful in this learning setting.

_____ Helping the student determine a reward for acceptable behavior that really is a reward to him; e.g., teacher and student might agree that if assigned work is completed correctly before the end of the class period, the student will be allowed to play a game that he likes with a friend in the class, or he will be given a token that can be traded in for a bar of candy or, when five tokens are collected, for six bars of candy.

_____ Setting up a situation that allows the student to experience good behavior; e.g., the teacher might reduce the amount of assigned work for this student at the beginning of the behavior modification plan so that he can succeed with it. Later, as he develops improved habits of independent seat work, the assignments can be made longer if the teacher feels this is appropriate.

_____ Helping the student discriminate between acceptable and unacceptable behavior; e.g., the student may have *most* of his assigned work finished and ask the teacher if he can have the agreed-on reward. The teacher would remind him that this was not what the two of them had agreed on as being acceptable.

_____ Helping a student associate his appropriate behavior with the reward; e.g., the teacher would remind the student when letting him play a game that he is getting to do so because he has done assigned work well.

_____ Discussing a change in the reward if variety is needed; e.g., the student might be dropping back to his old habits. If so, a different reward might be selected.

_____ Complimenting the student on how well he is doing when the agreed-on reward is presented; e.g., the teacher might make specific reference to what he achieved today while giving him the reward for his success.

_____ Evaluating the changed behavior of the student; e.g., the teacher might record again the frequency of the behavior that is the focus of the plan. This will help the teacher set an objective picture of how well the plan is working with the student.

_____ Helping the student to be able to give up the extrinsic reward and to function in the regular classroom setting as well as other settings; e.g., the teacher would help the student to understand that he can work independently and can successfully accomplish his assigned work without the motivation of a reward.

SOME ADVANTAGES
The following are often mentioned as advantages of the behavior modification strategy:

- It builds on the natural behavior of many concerned teachers who have been using social incentives of a positive nature throughout their teaching careers; e.g., praise of a child either in writing or verbally when he does something well, for the purpose of encouraging the child to continue this specific behavior.

- It elicits a rapid response from students, because the reward incentive often gives them immediate gratification; e.g., food, a chance to play a game they like, knowlege that they have achieved in learning what they set out to learn.

- The strategy can be used to help students achieve academic success as well as to improve behavior that has created problems in the learning setting.

- It reduces curriculum demands in many programs to pupil ability, ensuring success, while interest is maintained by presenting the requirements to the students in small bits for the purpose of conditioning against failure.

- The method requires teachers to clearly specify the type of behavior that is acceptable in the learning setting, because the behavior of students who have problems is being modified to be acceptable.

- The method eliminates the necessity for extrinsic rewards after it becomes evident that pupils can learn; e.g., often children who have not succeeded previously find that success in learning can be its own reward.

SOME DISADVANTAGES
The following are often mentioned as disadvantages of the behavior modification strategy:

- It is often viewed as a method to be used only with behavior problems, because it has had its greatest use with disruptive students.

- It is regarded by some teachers of older students as a "gimmick" that can only be used with younger children.

- It could cause some teachers and administrators to try to modify students' behavior so that they would adapt to an unexciting curriculum, rather than trying to create a stimulating environment for learning.

- There is fear that the student would never move from the motivation created by the extrinsic-reward stage and that he would expect teachers to use this strategy with him throughout his educational program.

- It can involve purchasing rewards, and teachers who begin to purchase the rewards from their own money might find that they are unable to continue to do so. (The money for rewards, of course, usually comes from school funds.)

- The strategy makes it difficult for teachers who are often accustomed to punishing misbehavior to adjust to a procedure where good behavior is rewarded.

- It may hinder the proper rewarding of some students who have been behavior problems, for they have been receiving a definite psychological reward from the attention they get from the teacher and students for bad behavior.

- The strategy causes some students to be rewarded while others are not. This creates a situation in which the student whose behavior has been good without a reward wonders why the child who has misbehaved previously is being rewarded for good behavior.

- It gives students an unrealistic picture of life, because society does not ignore misbehavior or give rewards to help people improve their behavior.

CLASSROOM EXAMPLE (ELEMENTARY)

Rather than looking at only one group of children working with their teachers, let us take a tour of a school and examine some of the behavior modification practices that may be observed:

1. A child has just completed reading an original story to the teacher, who praises her on her creativity.

2. A teacher is setting up a contract with a child. The contract is for him to complete a social studies project. If he completes all that he says he plans to do in the contract to the satisfaction of himself and the teacher, he will receive the best grade in social studies that he has ever had.

3. A child is using a set of programed materials that give him immediate knowledge of his progress as he moves through each step.

4. A teacher is writing a note to be taken home to a child's parent. The child has been particularly helpful in class today, although he is usually quite disruptive. The note praises the boy on his good behavior and compliments the child and the parent for the helpful gestures performed by the boy during the day.

5. A child is using a new set of materials that contains a worksheet with a chemical means of changing color when the child marks the correct answer.

6. The teacher is ignoring the bad behavior of a girl but complimenting the good behavior of another child in front of the total group.

7. The teacher has just told two children who have been having difficulty in spelling and have needed her special help that if they spell all words correctly on the weekly test, they will get a new box of crayons.

8. A teacher is having a conference with a child to discuss why she is not achieving the success at school that she and the teacher would like.

9. A teacher and his class are making plans for a new literature study. The children are helping to establish the goals and objectives of the unit of study. He is placing their suggestions and ideas on the board for the consideration of the total class.

10. A child has been isolated from the rest of the group and is sitting in a corner of the room facing the wall.

11. The children have just returned from a field trip and the teacher is complimenting them on how well they behaved.

12. A child is back at the listening table with earphones on, enjoying a favorite record. Her arithmetic assignment for the day has been completed and is correct. She and the teacher had agreed that if the work were done, she could listen to the record.

Analysis/Comment (Elementary)

As indicated earlier in this section, the competency worksheet for the behavior modification strategy was planned to illustrate how a teacher might go about preparing a master plan for behavioral change with a child or group of children. Because examples were used at each checkpoint to illustrate what this teacher behavior might look like in relation to one individual, it might be helpful to the reader to see other behaviors of teachers that could be classified as behavior modification, although all do not follow the steps indicated on the competency worksheet. Let us review each of the activities observed and analyze what is happening:

1. The teacher is using praise as a social incentive for the child who has written a creative original story. Most teachers use praise as a way of modifying behavior in a classroom, because it is easy and natural. A summary of the existing research related to praise indicates that when given at the time the specific desired behaviors were exhibited, it has proved effective in increasing these behaviors. The research also reveals, however, that some students are less responsive than others to praise and that some persons were more effective givers of praise than were others.

2. Contracts are becoming more frequently used in elementary schools as a way of motivating students to successfully achieve realistic objectives for themselves. The child in this case is trying to raise his grade in social studies, and he and the teacher agreed that if he accomplished the terms of the contract, he would receive a higher grade.

3. The incentive for this child to modify his behavior is the fact that he is receiving immediate feedback from the set of programed materials. He can modify his behavior to correct his responses, if he learns from the materials that they are incorrect. Research indicates that the student is the best judge of when information feedback should be given, because it is not always true that this type of immediate result helps a child to be successful. Sometimes it can interrupt and retard performance.

4. Here is another example of praise, but this time the teacher is putting it in writing and sending it home to the parents. (She probably needed to tell the boy what the note contained, because he has most likely taken home so many messages to his parents that told them of bad behavior that he might have been reluctant to deliver another one.) The principal of the school received a phone call from the mother of this child the next day. The mother said she was framing the note from the teacher, because it was the first time that she had ever received anything from the school saying something good about her child.

5. This is another use of the immediate feedback system, as illustrated in a rather sophisticated worksheet designed to let the child know how well he is doing. Materials of this type are appearing more and more on the commercial market and need to be carefully evaluated by teachers.

6. Here the teacher is complimenting a child for good behavior at the same time that another child is misbehaving. Her purpose is to cause the child who is not behaving to be motivated to seek the teacher's praise by modeling her behavior after the child being complimented. This is referred to as *vicarious reinforcement*, and although it has not been creatively tested in academic settings, those familiar with the field of behavior modification believe it to be a powerful and economical incentive device.

7. Here the teacher is using a material incentive to motivate two children who have been having difficulty with spelling and have received special help to be successful on the weekly test. She obviously knows from having worked with them closely that they can write the words correctly. The crayons, in her opinion, provide a more tangible reward and recognition of their successful learning experience. Material incentives, according to recent research, were less effective than expected in laboratory studies of certain types of learning. (In these studies, the timing, placement, or mode of delivery, rather than the type of incentive used, may have been responsible for lack of success.)

8. Here we see one step in the plan for developing an individual behavior modification program, as indicated on the list of checkpoints. The teacher is sharing some of her thoughts about the girl's behavior and is helping the

child think through ways in which she might become more successful in the school environment.

9. This teacher obviously believes that by involving children in the initial planning of an activity, they will be more likely to want to accomplish the objectives successfully. Because the long-range goal of behavior modification programs is to develop learners who are able to see the intrinsic rewards in learning and thus become better managers of their own learning, this planning session reveals one way in which a teacher can help students move toward that goal. Research does support the idea that if students are actively involved in managing their learning activities, they are more highly motivated and have better attitudes toward what they are doing.

10. Here we see an example of disapproval and punishment as a way of modifying behavior. The child has been isolated from the rest of the group and placed in a corner of the room facing the wall. The teacher probably tried to ignore the child's behavior, but became so frustrated by it that she placed him in a place where he would not disturb her or the children. Probably the next step would have been the principal's office had the child not calmed down and adjusted to working in the classroom. Most proponents of behavior modificaton advocate the use of positive rather than negative incentives, because of the more predictable effects of positive reinforcement. In cases where punishment is used, however, research appears to support the procedure of delivering it automatically and without emotional overtones.

11. This, of course, is another example of praise by the teacher. The children are being complimented on how well they behaved on a field trip. Often teachers forget to let children know when they have done something well and, instead, focus too much on the negative. This teacher obviously believes that praise can have a very positive effect in modifying the behavior of a group.

12. The child listening to the favorite record in this example is doing something that she likes to do, after having done something that she did not like to do as well. This is an example of *high probability behavior* (what a child is most likely to do) serving as a reinforcer for *low probability behavior* (what a child is most likely not to do). Current research reveals that this approach to behavior modification, hypothesized and investigated by Premack, can have great utility for children in school settings.

These twelve examples of behavior modification techniques in action in an elementary school reveal the variety of ways in which this strategy is often used.

There are still many questions and concerns about behavior modification, but one of the purposes of this book is to help the reader to look at the various strategies more carefully and to raise questions about them. One statement, however, that has helped us to come a bit closer to understanding why the use of behavior modification has become so popular in the real world of the classroom comes from Madsen and Madsen. They write as follows:

> Traditional teaching takes it for granted that children can be motivated from the beginning by teacher approval. In many cases it's true. But it doesn't work for the problem children, both the ones you notice and those you don't. You must start with the child where he is. You motivate him by what will work, not by what you think ought to work.[7]

Hopefully, this section on behavior modification and the examples above will cause you to begin thinking about this strategy more objectively, so that you can reject or accept parts of it on the basis of its weaknesses and strengths, as judged by your own study and experience.

CLASSROOM EXAMPLE (SECONDARY)

Certainly the instructional methods of which we write are appropriate for teaching teachers as well as teaching pupils. In normal classroom sessions with undergraduates in education, praise can be used to increase an analytical capability on the part of students. The following transcript was taped in the last few minutes of class, during which one of the authors discussed grading with his students:

TEACHER: I'm returning to you in a few minutes the "Dozen" papers you've turned in recently. Remember that on each paper you'll find a number indicating the accuracy of skills—for example, you may have received a score of 9. You may work some more on the skills, if you wish, until you achieve a level of mastery with which you are comfortable.

STUDENT 1: But there's no letter grade on this paper, right?

TEACHER: Right. That's solid inductive thinking, based on some of the things I've said lately about grading.

STUDENT 2: And we can turn the paper in again for a higher total, even keep doing it until we get a 12?

TEACHER: Some accurate listening on your part! Yes, if you wish. Any reason why not? What are we really after with this assignment?

STUDENT 1: A passing grade.

STUDENT 3: Gaining competence in the skills, I guess.

TEACHER: OK, competence. That's good. Being able to consciously and deliberately choose and employ certain precise skills to increase effectiveness of interpersonal communication—if you want it in an "official" nutshell. But your version is fine. So, if we are after that, how does the continuous feedback system help?

STUDENT 3: Well, it keeps the doors open. With the number total we have a kind of intrapersonal competition, if we want it. And the opportunity to work further on the skills and get continuous feedback from you on how we are doing helps us. A grade or at least the "one-time" type of teacher response tends to make us feel an assignment is "done," regardless of our personal level of competence with it.

TEACHER: Again, some critical reasoning on your part. I'm glad to hear you analyzing as you are. But for whom are you speaking?

STUDENT 3: For me.

TEACHER: Just checking. Have you all come to this kind of position?

STUDENT 1: No. I'd like to see you do both; give us the number right and a letter grade.

TEACHER: There's a thought!

STUDENT 1: You know, I've really been thinking about doing what you are using with us when I do my student teaching. But I'd like to use both the letter grade and the competency idea.

TEACHER: What else am I using—as you put it—on you.

STUDENT 2: Praise.

TEACHER: Aha!

STUDENT 2: You're using praise to help us think about grading.

TEACHER: To help you reason analytically about grading or anything else for that matter, to help you improve your critical thinking ability.

STUDENT 4: Speaking of that, I think it would work to keep the letter grade *and* the "competency number" *and* the continued self-improvement route. Both for us and for the kids we might teach.

STUDENT 1: That sounds good

TEACHER: It does to me, as well. Now, as a group, you're asking me to continue to indicate the number of skills you've worked with accurately, and, in addition, to assign a letter grade to your effort, *and* to maintain an open-door policy

	so that you can redo the paper if you choose—improving your competencies, and, incidentally, getting a higher letter grade in the process. Am I right?
STUDENT 3:	You used a paraphrase on us!
TEACHER:	An excellent process-awareness observation on your part. Good. Is it an accurate paraphrase? Am I on your wavelength regarding these options you'd like?
STUDENT 5:	Yes. Could this really be done in our public school classes? Along the lines Dan mentioned he was thinking?
TEACHER:	What do you think?
STUDENT 6:	We're already doing it in our field experiences' school. My cooperating teacher sends to parents a performance report card in each subject. The card has a list of pertinent competencies and those that the student can do and that the teacher has evidence of his doing, are checked. Then the school also sends home a letter grade.
STUDENT 5:	Does your school permit a student to continue to work with a paper or project until he can show a higher competency level and/or get a higher grade?
STUDENT 6:	No, actually I don't think they've thought of trying that. Nor did I before today. It would theoretically give all students an *A* wouldn't it?
TEACHER:	If all students did get an *A*, what would that mean?
STUDENT 7:	Let me try a thought. It might mean all students had learned the objectives you, the teacher, had set for them to learn—to the standard you had set for them based on their individual needs and abilities.
TEACHER:	Good reasoning and an interesting idea.
STUDENT 1:	That's not a bad outcome, in my opinion. I guess I've been hung up on the normal curve and equal distribution bit, and all that.
TEACHER:	Well, there is a lot more to "evaluating and grading" than what we've talked about so far. But at least with regard to grading, I've appreciated your comments and views. You seem to be keeping open to new ideas and analyzing both the new ones and the old ones. Also, it seems to me that some of you, at any rate, might have an interest in testing for yourselves in your schools both the use of praise to change behavior and the continuous feedback system for grading and evaluating that I use with you. If you want a value judgment from me, I'd say—that's great! Let's call it for the day at this point.

Analysis/Comment (Secondary)

Nothing especially dramatic occurs in the example just offered, and that is an important point to be made. Behavior modification, as a strategy, can be employed by the professional teacher in his routine work with students. It does, however, need to be seen for what it is and to be employed wittingly for a predetermined purpose. In the example, that purpose was to use praise to increase student ability to reason critically and logically—in a word, analytically.

Generally, behavior modification as a strategy works better, or at least outcomes are more discernible, if the teacher works with a student or a small group. Here, the strategy was used in relation to an entire class. In addition, the constellation of "analytical thinking" was chosen rather than, as the checkpoints suggest, one specific behavioral component thereof that students could exhibit. The job is harder as a result. It is, for instance, more difficult to observe closely the analytical thinking students are demonstrating in general or to pick up the absence of such behaviors than it is to observe and measure the more specific "ability to compare."

Again with reference to the checkpoints, the "reward" that the teacher is consciously fostering seems like an extrinsic one. He expects that his praise and reinforcement of any analytical reasoning demonstrated by students will make them feel good; a kind of reward in itself is to achieve teacher praise—he hopes that students will want teacher praise and will "think analytically" to get it. But even more importantly, he is counting on the satisfaction from reasoning clearly being its own reward—a personal one that is independent of teacher praise. Such a reward seems to accrue, for example, to the student who recognized the use of a paraphrase, to the one who first spotted "praise" at work, and to the one who "reasons out" a new idea relative to what an *A* might mean. As a part of consistent reinforcement, by the way, and in line with the behavior modification strategy, note that the teacher ignored the "wise crack" response to the question, "What are we really after?" but rewarded the following comment that is backgrounded in more critical thinking. Then, too, he constructively (and gently) criticized the student who used "we" to express an idea that seemed to be his alone. An implied suggestion that the student speak for himself, at least until he assesses others' beliefs, is itself reinforcing to the overall goal of helping students strengthen their skills of analytical reasoning.

Toward the end of the dialogue, students are encouraged to try the idea of continuous feedback, with options, in their own field experience situations. At least one student expressed interest in so doing. In these generally supportive school settings, students could have a reasonable amount of time to experience "good" behavior. That is, they could practice praising pupils in a discussion on grading (as in the example) or whatever, under the guidance of the cooperating teacher, or they could operate in an environment where the cooperating teacher uses praise as they might be expected to use it. Because they are *student* teachers, they can try without fear of immediate personal catastrophe and, thus, they have the opportunity to do well in using praise to reinforce desired behavior.

(They will continue to see a parallel in the class used in the example, of course, as the teacher provides continuing situations in which they can at least observe desired behavior; i.e., in this case, the warranted use of praise by a teacher who is attempting to modify the behavior of students toward the end of their being more analytical thinkers.)

Note that not much was done in the example in relation to the final three checkpoints. The idea of the worksheet is to help the teacher to be in a position to modify his behavior if he so chooses. It functions as a kind of self-directed behavior modification strategy. In this case, the teacher might agree that his use of the strategy is incomplete, and he might plan to try some things that would help his students discriminate between analytical (desirable behavior) and prejudiced thinking (undesirable behavior) on their part. Perhaps a continued use of praise, with the announced intention of giving it for evidenced aspects of analytical thinking *only* would work. Or the teacher could give each student a punch card, punch it when he or she exhibits analytical thinking, and allow a card fully "punched out" over five class sections, perhaps, to be turned in for an *A*. To grade-conscious college students such an idea may not be far-fetched at all. At least, then the teacher would have additional extrinsic motivation working toward a desirable goal. By the completion of his work with the students, however, it is to be hoped that they would have no need for punch cards or the like but would exhibit the desired behavior because they want to and because doing so is intellectually rewarding in its own right. The behavior modification strategy—through more complete attention to the teacher-oriented behaviors that comprise it—will have served well, then, as a worthy means to a desirable end.

NOTES

1. Clifford K. Madsen and Charles H. Madsen, Jr., "What Is Behavior Modification?" *Curriculum Planning: A New Approach*, Glen Hass, Joseph Bondi, and Jon Wiles (eds.), (Boston: Allyn and Bacon, 1974), p. 116.
2. John P. DeCecco and William R. Crawford, *The*

Psychology of Learning and Instruction (Englewood Cliffs, N.J.: Prentice-Hall, 1974), p. 5.

3. Ibid.

4. Sherman H. Frey, "Teachers and Behavior Modification," *Phi Delta Kappan* LV (No. 9, May 1974), pp. 634-635.

5. Dewey Lipe and Steven H. Jung, "Manipulating Incentives to Enhance Learning," *Education Yearbook: 1972-73* (New York: Macmillan Co. and Free Press) pp. 35-34.

6. Madsen and Madsen, op. cit., p. 117.

7. Madsen and Madsen, op. cit., p. 121.

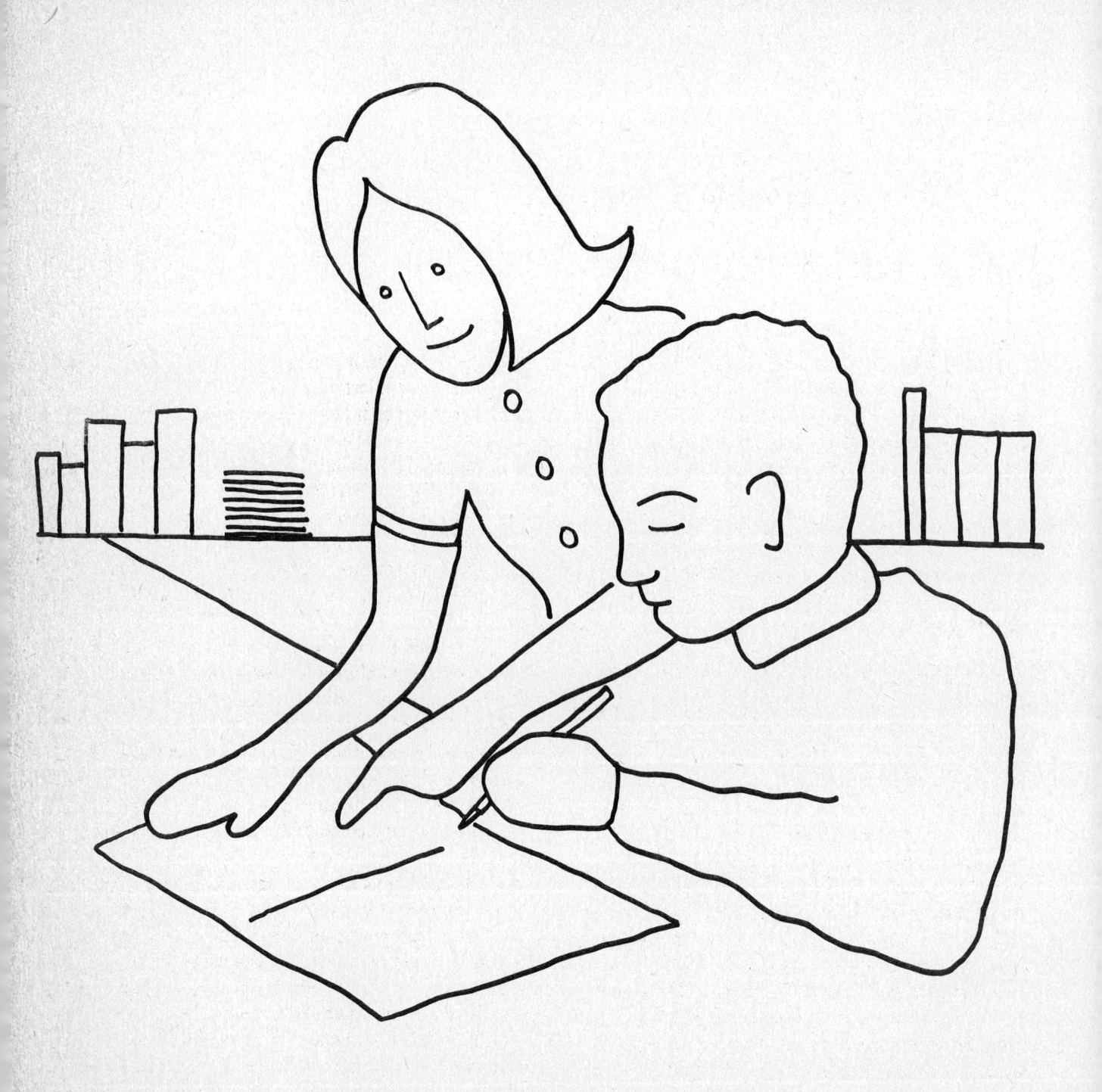

strategy 11

Performance-Based Learning Activity Packages

BACKGROUND
The rising public concern that educators bear increased accountability for the learning of students in our nation's schools has been one of the major forces in the emergence of *performance-based instruction* (also referred to as competency-based instruction).

Although much controversy has been associated with performance-based instruction, a precise definition has not been agreed on by American educators. We would like to share several statements that hopefully will clarify the meaning of performance-based instruction, however, because the increased use of learning activity packages is an outgrowth of this educational approach.

Quite concisely, Nagel and Richman define performance-based instruction as a "rather high-sounding collection of words that means in essence a flexible, individualized program that frees both students and teachers to work at their own rates without the fear of failure."[1]

Howsam expands this definition by pointing out that people who talk about performance-based instruction "are saying that the teacher-learning process is facilitated if the teacher knows what he wants the pupil to learn and if the learner is aware of precisely what is expected of him or what he expects of himself."[2] Howsam also writes that "the learner or teacher is most likely to do what is expected of him and what he expects of himself if he is accountable for doing what he undertakes."

The essential ingredients of performance-based instruction, again according to Howsam, are: "(a) precise objectives in behavioral terms; (b) performance criteria, indicators of performance, modes of assessment and criterion levels specified and made public along with objectives; (c) instruction pertinent to the criteria; and (d) learner accountability in terms of the criteria."[3]

In school systems where the pressure for increased accountability has resulted in a closer examination of performance-based instruction, teachers have been applying this approach to their traditional methods as well as developing new ones. One of these is the performance-based learning activity package (PBLAP), which is sometimes referred to as an instructional module (IM).

The PBLAP is a self-contained unit of instruction, usually in the form of a printed guide that directs and assists an individual toward precise behavioral objectives that are based on a careful analysis of the students' needs and abilities. The most dominant characteristic of the PBLAP, which is currently being used at both elementary and secondary levels, is that it provides variation—variation in ways of achieving the objectives and variation in the amount of time individuals spend on the package. The packages are also designed so that if the student does not achieve the agreed-on goals, he may then involve himself in additional activities until the objective has been reached. The packages are designed to provide an individualized learning experience for students and may be planned cooperatively by the student and teacher.

Our review of a variety of learning activity packages and materials that have been planned to help teachers use this strategy has revealed that most packages include the following eight components:

1. *Prerequisites.* These include requirements to be completed prior to beginning the package, as well as background information to establish rationale for the package and to review procedures for its use.
2. *Pre-assessment.* This is a means of determining if the package is needed by the individual student.
3. *Objectives.* Packages may contain both instructional and expressive objectives. *Instructional objectives* are written in behavioral terms; each defines what is to be demonstrated, the conditions under which it is to be demonstrated, the level of acceptable performance, and the means of evaluation. (See Objective 1 in Abridged Learning Activity sample package, p. 116.) An *expressive objective* is one that does not necessarily result in specific behavioral changes but has the potential of contributing to the students appreciation. (See objective for Quest Activity One, p. 117.)
4. *Flow Chart.* Packages usually include graphic representation of how a student might progress through—or out of—the package.
5. *Instructional Activities.* Readings, use of multi-media materials, research, creative projects, and various other means of enabling the student to successfully complete the objectives of the package are other common components. The student should be able to choose from at least two options that lead to the same objectives. He may also plan with the teacher other means of accomplishing the objectives, if another plan would be more appropriate for his individual learning style.
6. *Post-assessment.* This component is a means of determining if the student has established competency in relation to the agreed-on objectives of the package.
7. *Remediation.* Additional activities for the student who has not yet achieved mastery of the performance objective are also important. The package may contain additional activities for this purpose, or the teacher may plan these with the student.
8. *Resources.* A listing of materials needed for accomplishing the performance objectives of the package is an additional aspect of most packages.

One of the basic beliefs of performance-based instruction is that most students can become competent at almost anything if given enough time. Learning activity packages reflect this belief; when correctly used, achievement remains constant while time varies; i.e., each student is given enough time to learn whatever is required of him in the package.[4]

Several years ago, Mitzel wrote that we are on the brink of an "impending instruction revolution" in which learning will increasingly be defined as a way of characterizing change in a student's behavior in some desired direction between two definite time markers.[5] The teacher who wants to keep up with the changing scene in educational strategies can hardly afford to ignore performance-based instruction as represented in the learning activity package strategy.

COMPETENCY WORKSHEET FOR PLANNING AND OBSERVING

Checkpoints

Observer Notes

When using the performance-based learning activity package strategy, the teacher is usually observed performing the following behaviors:

_____ Diagnosing children's needs and abilities.

_____ Preparing packages, based on his diagnosis, that usually include the following eight components: (1) prerequisites, (2) pre-assessment, (3) objectives, (4) flow chart, (5) instructional activities, (6) post-assessment, (7) remediation, and (8) resources.

_____ Describing management procedures, including time recommendations for involving the pupils in the use of the packets; e.g., informing pupils that they must check in with the teacher at the beginning of each class session and should work to meet the suggested time guidelines as best they can.

_____ Clarifying with each student the work to be accomplished either individually or as a group; e.g., students are able to select learning packages that best meet their needs as they pursue the competencies.

_____ Functioning as a counselor and supervisor.

_____ Making materials available in sufficient quality and number.

_____ Evaluating pre-assessment activities.

_____ Permitting and encouraging pupils to work outside of

the classroom—at home, in the media center, or in the library, for instance.

_____ Providing feedback to the student concerning his performance on the objectives of the package and the relationship of his performance to his overall achievement within the class.

_____ Revising, as needed, the learning activity packages so that they are appropriate for the students using them.

_____ Giving appropriate encouragement to the student as he works to achieve the agreed-on objectives of the package.

SOME ADVANTAGES
The following are often mentioned as some of the advantages of the performance-based learning activity package strategy:

- Though tightly designed, the performance-based learning activity package strategy is actually planned so that teaching may be individualized for assisting students or small groups of students to achieve predetermined outcomes. For example, packages include several different routes, which allow students to work in their own cognitive styles and at their own levels of ability in achieving an objective.

- The PBLAP strategy enables students to work at their own rates. Slower students may be given more time on a particular learning activity package, for example. And all students can be encouraged to spend more time on those tasks that are more difficult for them and less time on tasks in which they are competent.

- The method requires individualization, self-pacing, and evaluation without comparison with others, thus increasing the pupils' pleasure and motivation.

- The strategy stipulates individualization of instruction which requires a diagnostic approach to teaching. For example, a teacher would need to assess the interests, needs, and abilities of his students before and during his work with the strategy.

- The PBLAP strategy does much to remove the fear of failure from the learning environment. Students are not classified as failures simply because they are unable to achieve the desired level of competency; instead, the teacher works with the student until the desired competency has been reached.

- It offers a more organized approach to instruction than do some other methods. With a package, the student is given a great deal of responsibility for his own learning and yet he gets specific help from the package to guide him. Self-checks in the package, for example, enable him to determine where he is and whether he is going toward the agreed-on goals.

- Because use of the PBLAP strategy provides clearly discernible results of student mastery or lack thereof at a given time, it helps teachers take a careful look at what their teaching is designed to accomplish, and it requires them to review carefully and to modify, as appropriate, the way they go about accomplishing their objectives.

- This strategy encourages teacher and student creativity in developing packages for instruction and in modifying existing packages for greater effectiveness.

- The PBLAP strategy provides teachers with the freedom to participate actively and on an individual basis with students—as counselors and enablers of learning, for example.

- The strategy contributes to a kind of self-fulfilling prophecy, because the pupil and the teacher have agreed on realistic objectives that the teacher believes the pupil can accomplish successfully. Because the teacher expects a student to succeed, the student is more likely to do so.

SOME DISADVANTAGES

The following are often mentioned as some of the disadvantages of the performance-based learning activity package strategy:

- The strategy could be viewed by students, colleagues, parents—and even the teachers—as a factory-line approach to instruction that is inconsistent with the traditional role of the teacher as the sole distributor of knowledge.

- The strategy utilizes self-paced instruction and evaluation procedures, and pupils who have not had previous experience with learning activity packages are often slow to adjust.

- The strategy requires that a considerable amount of time be given to developing the packages in preparation for using it. Additional teacher time is also spent in supervising and counseling students to help them work successfully with the learning activity packages.

- The strategy might discourage teachers, once packages have been prepared, from doing much modification from year to year to meet the changing needs and interests of students.

- The strategy requires very careful supervision; the independent nature of the learning activities could allow the teacher to lose contact with children who are unchallenged by the package or are too shy to ask for help.

- The strategy might encourage students to see a particular skill or competency as *only* an end in itself. With this perspective, once they have received their reward—a passing grade or whatever—they might be unlikely to continue in the particular type of behavior being developed by the package.

- It might discourage pupils who do not have the requisite reading or independent study skills.

- The strategy requires a change of traditional reporting practices, which are usually based on comparing students with each other. Such changes are often difficult to obtain.

CLASSROOM EXAMPLE
(ELEMENTARY AND SECONDARY)

The account that follows illustrates the PBLAP strategy in operation in an elective journalism class in a middle school. The example includes an abridged performance-based learning activity package provided the authors by a practicing teacher. (The paragraphs of the example have been keyed by numbers to the Analysis/Comment that follows.)

The teacher began as follows:

(1) "For today, people, we are going to learn more about how news stories are written. Those of you who have been scheduled to work with reading should be getting your group together, your files out, picking up the reading materials from their regular place, and getting started, as best you can. Work in a group around my desk. Your assignment is on the board. You'll be reading materials about newspapers and reporters. I'll call you together later for a session with me, when we can also see if you are ready for trying the packages that the others will be using.

"The rest of you will be working on learning activity packages for the next five days. I'm going to give you all the information you'll need to get started right now. The packages will give you specific objectives to be accomplished and will direct you into activities for accomplishing them. By the time we are done, you'll be able to tell your folks or anyone else just how a news story is written, as well as to write your own without any help. I might add that in the near future you will be writing a news story for our school newspaper.

(2) "You'll recall we've been talking about what makes news and the need and responsibility for accuracy in reporting; that gives us some appropriate background for getting into the skills of actually writing a story. The talk was fine and helpful, but it has done its job and we're at the point, now, where we need to both analyze and produce stories if we are really going to learn newswriting—which, in turn, is crucial to an understanding and appreciation of journalism.

(3) "You'll be working with the learning activity packages on the tables around the sides of the room. (Note: See the abridged sample package at the end of this Classroom Example, p. 115.) Packages are self-directing and are to be worked on individually. See me if you have any questions or need any help. Each of you must read the background and take the pre-assessment test in the package with the yellow cover. Our aide will check the answers to your pre-assessment tests. If you pass the test, you can go to the package with the green cover and take the test there. If you don't pass the test in the yellow package, then read the objectives and choose one of the options for achieving the objectives. If you pass the assessment test in the green package, come see me. I'll serve as 'publisher,' which means that anyone showing competency above and beyond what is in the green package is eligible for a special enrichment assignment. There are also some special assignments—'quest assignments' I've called them—in both the yellow and green packages. I'll tell you more about these and help you with them on an individual basis. Now, let's see if you have any questions; then, you should go to work. Be sure to check with me, especially as you finish your package."

(4) After dealing with a few general questions, the teacher visited the reading group that was seated in a circle by his desk to be sure that each student was working on self-directed materials that could help him overcome his reading difficulties.

(5) While this was going on, the other students started looking into the yellow and green packets. As soon as the teacher felt he could leave the reading group, he began to move around the room. He told one boy to put a newspaper he was reading back in the pile at the rear of the room and get started on the day's assignment. He observed one girl beginning to work with a green package; he thought she would be more successful in a yellow one, so he told her to move to a yellow package. On his return to the reading group, he responded individually to a student who asked if he could join the others, by saying, "Yes, you can try the yellow package, but I'd recommend you first build up your reading ability even further; the reading progress chart in your file shows you might have difficulties."

(6) The other students, meanwhile, continued to work with various packages around the room, as they chose. Sufficient numbers of the yellow and green packages were available to eliminate any need for grabbing, complaining, or sharing. At this point, one student informed the teacher that she had taken the post-assessment in the yellow learning activity package. She showed the teacher her post-assessment news story. He noted that it was lacking in some essential ingredients of a news lead. Together they discussed the omissions and the reasons why she had not satisfactorily met the objectives. Following this, the teacher suggested she try the other activity option in the yellow package. The teacher reminded the student that she would not receive credit for being able to write a news story until she learned how to write the lead satisfactorily. Looking rather displeased, the girl went back to her desk. Another student stated he had finished the yellow package. The teacher's observation supported this contention, at which point the teacher reviewed with the student what he might do next. For example, he could do the quest activities in the yellow package or he could take the pre-assessment test in the green package.

(7) As the class drew to a close, the teacher informed his students that packages might be

taken home and that tomorrow they would continue what had been started in this day's session. Thursday, he reminded them, would be the weekly class meeting, at which time they would have an opportunity to offer feedback on the PBLAP method from their viewpoint as well as any comments they might wish to offer on how they were doing as individuals learning to write news stories. At this point, the class concluded.

The following is an abridged version of the yellow package being used in the example.

AN ABRIDGED LEARNING ACTIVITY PACKAGE

Cover

Learning Activity Package
Newswriting
Grades 6-8

Page One

Background

The overall goal of this package is to help you develop ability to know what makes up a news story as well as how to write one yourself.

Throughout your school years, you have probably had extensive work in writing papers, poems, and letters. In this package, you will learn another style of writing—one you come into contact with every day through the newspaper; newswriting. You might keep in mind as you work that the systematic pattern of a news story works much like a computer in placing the parts of a story into their slots. Your job as the writer is to know the parts and the pattern, and to investigate and provide the necessary information and skills for both to fit together.

Writing is, after all, a method of communicating oneself to others—whether it be through feelings or experiences. Newswriting, however, is primarily concerned with informing others from an *objective* viewpoint. Because of the speed of daily occurrences and the competition among media to relate them, a news story must be accurate, reasonably complete, and to the point. You should find yourself paying close attention to the need for every idea and sentence you use in your writing; each must merit its use. The techniques used in writing news stories are helpful, also, in writing letters, reports, and the like—even creative fiction.

If you believe you presently have the ability to write a news story, turn to the pre-assessment test. If you pass this test, then you have successfully achieved the objectives of this package. If you do not pass the pre-assessment test, return to this page and continue reading.

There are two routes or options you can follow to achieve the objectives of this package. Look through them and then choose one. You are advised to complete the option you start; however, you may go to another option if you have real difficulties. If you like, you may do both options in this package and also the quest activities. Please consult the teacher for help whenever you wish. You may take the post-assessment test, if you feel you have reached mastery of the objective. Remember, you must be able to show to the teacher you have fulfilled the objectives of the package before you can exit.

Pre-assessment Test
Perhaps you have already had some experience in the field of newswriting. Your results on this test will determine whether or not you must complete this package. You must achieve at least 80 percent

accuracy on this pre-test to waive the lessons in the package; if you do not achieve 80 percent or better, you are asked to continue with the package. The test should also serve the purpose of giving you some insight into information you will be learning if you work through the instructional package. Upon completion of the test, take your answer sheet to the teacher where you and he will grade and evaluate it.

Pre-assessment Item
1. List the six essential ingredients of a news lead.

Objectives
1. During a classroom session, the student will be able to list at least four of the six essential elements of a complete news lead. The teacher will check this list for accuracy.

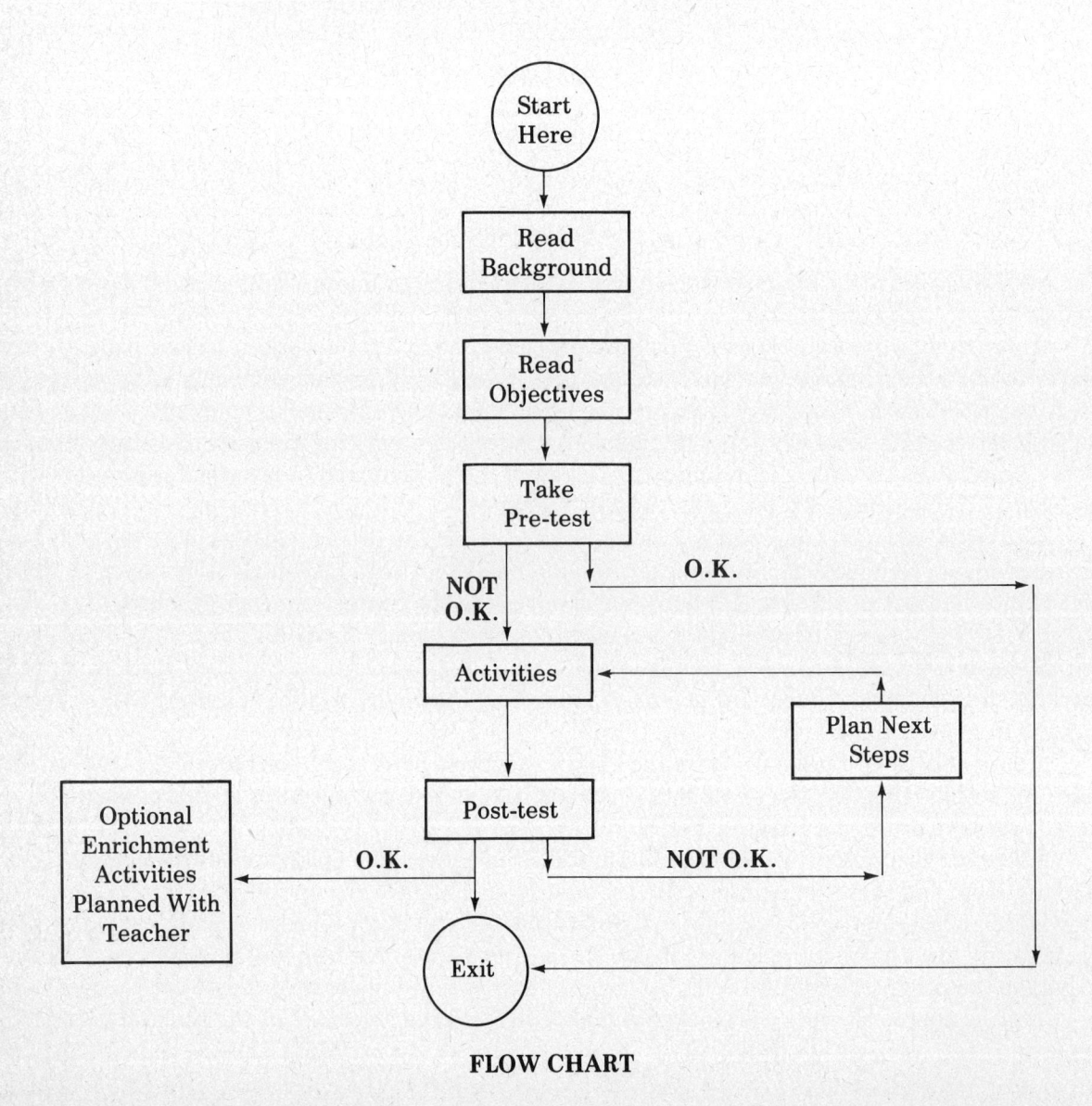

```
                    ┌───────┐
                    │ Start │
                    │ Here  │
                    └───┬───┘
                        ↓
                  ┌──────────┐
                  │  Read    │
                  │Background│
                  └────┬─────┘
                       ↓
                  ┌──────────┐
                  │  Read    │
                  │Objectives│
                  └────┬─────┘
                       ↓
                  ┌──────────┐
                  │  Take    │
                  │ Pre-test │
                  └────┬─────┘
           NOT O.K.    │          O.K.
                       ↓                   →→→→→→→→→→→
                  ┌──────────┐
                  │Activities│←──────────┐
                  └────┬─────┘           │
                       ↓             ┌───┴────┐
                                     │Plan Next│
                  ┌──────────┐       │ Steps  │
                  │Post-test │       └───┬────┘
                  └─┬──────┬─┘           ↑
            O.K.   │      │   NOT O.K.
   ┌──────────┐    │      │
   │ Optional │←───┘      └──────────→
   │Enrichment│
   │Activities│
   │Planned With│
   │  Teacher │
   └──────────┘
                       ↓
                    ┌──────┐
                    │ Exit │←────
                    └──────┘
```

FLOW CHART

Instructional Activities

Option One
In the rear of the classroom is a projector with headphones and a screen. View the short film on writing a news story. Pay close attention to the presentation of the *6 W's*. What are they? Why are they needed?

After you have finished the film viewing, go on with this activity as directed below....

[*Note:* The rest of the activity could have some self-tests to help the learner assess his progress before he reaches the final test. The same would be true for the second activity that follows.]

Option Two
Read the chapter in our text on newswriting. Pay attention to the discussion of the inverted pyramid style. Why was it adopted for the arrangement of a news story? What are the *6 W's?* Why are they needed? After you have finished reading, go on with the activity as directed below.

Quest Activities
If you wish to go further into the writing of news stories, you are invited to do so upon the satisfactory attainment on your part of all objectives of this package. You may do any of the following quest activities, or, if you desire, you may come up with your own optional quest activity. However, if you have your own idea for a quest activity, clear it with the teacher before beginning. In all cases, work out the initiating and the completing of quest activities with the teacher.

Quest Activity One
The objective of this activity is to help yourself to find out more about how news stories are written and what happens to them after they are written, by visiting the city newspaper office. Watch the people at work. Watch the putting together of the newspaper. Try to follow a story from when it is assigned to a reporter to its appearance in print. It is best to call in advance and ask to be given a tour so that you might be better able to do this quest activity.

Post-assessment
Upon completing at least one of the activities in this package, you may proceed to the post-test that follows. Read the directions and questions carefully. When you finish, take your answer paper to the teacher for evaluating. If you receive 80 percent or better, you have completed this package successfully.

Post-assessment Item
1. Using the facts below, write a journalistically "correct" news lead. You need not use all the information if it is not pertinent to the lead. Date it today.

Remediation
[*Note:* If the student does not achieve success as evidenced by the post-test, he and the teacher will confer in order to map out a course of action to improve performance before the student takes a second post-assessment. In some cases, the student's performance on the post-assessment may cause the teacher to recommend a package that is less difficult for him before coming back to this one. In other cases, a student may need additional help even after the second post-assessment in order to successfully complete the package.

Resources

1. Daily newspapers; different kinds if possible
2. Class textbook
3. 16mm. film projector
4. Film on writing a news story

Analysis/Comment

Some basic points of critique can be made in connection with the use of the PBLAP strategy described in this Classroom Example, which serves for both elementary and secondary.

For instance, in his opening remarks (1), the teacher tells his students what they will be able to do when they complete their learning package. A bit of rationale is given in the background section of the yellow packet, but generally the reason *why* students are learning to write news stories is not provided verbally by the teacher, although he does say they will soon be writing stories for the school newspaper.

From the directions given by the teacher (3) and the procedures stated in the remainder of the background material, it seems that the teacher expects most of his students to move toward the specified objectives successfully under his guidance. Moreover, he probably has some prior knowledge that his students need the competencies he has set out to teach. Evidence to suggest this is provided by his requiring "average" students to do the packages, while slower readers are working on reading skills. Students gaining the required competencies will be offered enrichment assignments. A suggestion would be to also offer these more accomplished students a chance to revise present packages and develop new ones. Also in the area of initiating the use of the packages, it might have been helpful to this teacher if he had set up some definite agreement with *all* his students concerning what they planned to accomplish—by means of contracts, for example. To illustrate how a contract might have been helpful, both he and the student who went to the green packet first (5) would have had in writing specifically that she would complete the yellow package pre-assessment first.

Once things get under way, the teacher does serve as an enabler or learning supervisor-counselor. While doing this, however, he reveals a minor "contradiction" (5). Although his stated objective is to help students to write newspaper stories, he tells the boy reading—of all things, a newspaper—to put it back and, in effect, to get back to thinking about newswriting only through the use of the packet. The teacher's ego involvement in developing the packages has possibly caused him to lose sight of the fact that there are various approaches a student could use to reach the objectives of the package.

On the whole, from observing the behavior of the students and from listening to the teacher's comments, it is evident that both teacher and pupils realize a workable administrative plan has been developed and implemented and that both parties are functioning by it quite smoothly. The background information and the flow chart both help make the plan clearer. An interesting point for observing close adherence to the flow chart occurs when the boy (6) who has successfully completed his initial work and passed the post-assessment test plans with the teacher what he might do as optional enrichment activities.

Materials for pupil work are plentiful—evidently clearly written, because no pupil complaints or confusions are recorded in the example—and these materials have obviously been written for at least two levels of achievement. Again, personalized contracts could be added to the teaching plan, to ensure that each student has a packet that has been modified to fit his individual needs and abilities.

Finally, in analyzing the strategy in the classroom example given, teachers who plan to use the PBLAP strategy might well consider the provisions for the receiving and giving of feedback such as this teacher has built in through the class meeting technique (7) Feedback is of particular significance in the case of this teacher, who offered very little verbal support for the students in the example.

In sum, this teacher provided a "tie-in" for students with previous work; he informed them of the general objective of the class (newswriting) and their more specific job (writing a news story on their own); he seemed to be trying—successfully, by and large—to teach through what may well be for him a strategy with which he does not yet feel fully comfortable. His willingness to let students work on the packages at their own pace, but with supervision and accountability to him, suggests that he is in agreement with the major thrusts of the philosophy behind the PBLAP strategy. With increased usage of the strategy, the teacher would hopefully be able to guide the students to a greater awareness of the need for being accountable to themselves for their own learning; this, of course, is one of the goals of education.

NOTES

1. Thomas S. Nagel and Paul T. Richman, *Competency-Based Instruction: A Strategy to Eliminate Failure* (Columbus, Ohio: Charles E. Merrill, 1972), p. 1.

2. Robert B. Howsam, "Some Basic Concepts," *Today's Education* (April 1972), p. 3 of special section.

3. Ibid.

4. Nagel and Richman, op. cit., pp. 3, 73.

5. Harold E. Mitzel, "The Impending Instruction Revolution," *Phi Delta Kappan* (April 1970), pp. 434-439.

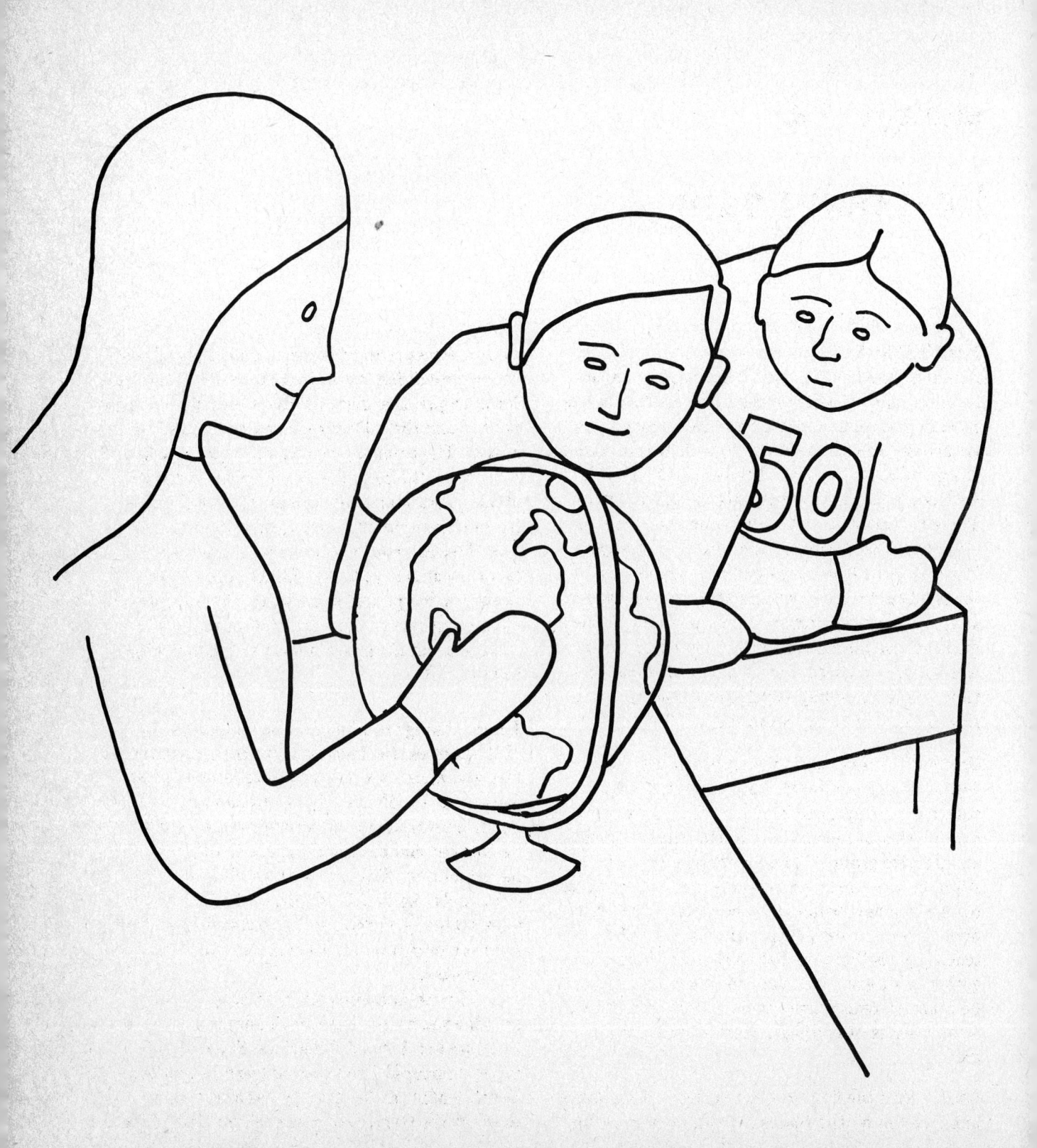
50

strategy 12

Do-Look-Learn

BACKGROUND

Although the name of this strategy may be new to some, parts of it are commonly used by many teachers. Both elementary and secondary teachers across the nation, in our experience, frequently ask students to join in small groups to work with some project or task to facilitate learning. These teachers have at least begun the method. The complete version of the strategy, however, involves three teacher-guided operations. Although the strategy has emerged in recent years as a popular one for working with adults, teachers have also adopted it for effective use at the elementary and secondary level. Some elaboration on the three key words more readily clarifies the strategy and its purposes:

Do. The teacher creates an opportunity that will provide a common "here and now" experience for a group or several groups. (A group may be two or more; three to six students make an effective group.) The emphasis is on doing! All members have a chance to engage in activities, to practice new behaviors, and to increase their own learning from the specific task that the teacher gives them or that they have planned together. For example, a group of students may be asked to read an incomplete story and then write a series of endings generated from the group.

Look. With the help of the teacher and/or someone selected by the teacher, group members look at themselves as they prepare to do the task and as they are doing the task. Before doing the task, for example, the students might look at the skills needed and the talents represented within the group. The teacher provides time during which he and the students give and receive feedback about the task and the process of completing it. For example, they might describe and analyze their current behavior, make judgments about what is happening, reflect about why things are happening as they are, or conceptualize about one or more ways of improving their work in the group and/or in dealing with the task.

Learn. Along with helping the students look at themselves, the teacher helps them to recognize and identify what they have learned or are learning to do differently. For example, they might discuss how any learnings gained could be adapted and modified for use in other, similar situations. The teacher may choose to use either aids (e.g., chalkboards, evaluation check sheets, tape recorders, group- or teacher-written reports) or simply verbal comment to assist in this process.

The method emerges from extensive research done by the National Training Laboratory Institute for Applied Behavioral Sciences into the ways people function and learn in groups. Development of the strategy has also been fostered by the Center for Research on Utilization of Scientific Knowledge, University of Michigan. In addition, the Northwest Regional Educational Laboratory, specifically Dr. John Wallen, worked on preparing and field testing the strategy for use in an educational setting. By December 1969, the catch phrase "Do-Look-Learn" had come to be affixed to a teaching strategy involving small groups that focus both on a learning objective and on the group processes involved in accomplishing that objective.[1] At present, the Northwest Regional Laboratory is conducting workshops demonstrating this method throughout the nation, for both elementary and secondary teachers. Research has also been initiated to determine its effectiveness.

In sum, whether the professional teacher is developing a specific skill, understanding, or attitude that is related to a particular discipline, or is aiding students to work effectively with their peers in small group efforts toward the completion of a task, he or she will find do-look-learn a viable teaching strategy.

COMPETENCY WORKSHEET FOR PLANNING AND OBSERVING

Checkpoints

Observer Notes

When using the do-look-learn strategy, the teacher is usually observed performing the following behaviors:

_____ Making plans for the group or groups; e.g., gathering and analyzing pertinent data in order to select appropriate tasks and schedule group sessions with or without student involvement.

_____ Organizing students into small groups.

_____ Informing the students of how they will work using this strategy; e.g., some may be given designated roles such as observer, helper, helpee.

_____ Helping the students identify and begin to do the agreed-on task.

_____ Conducting himself basically as a manager of the strategy; e.g., the teacher moves about the groups, assisting students in each stage of the strategy. The stages may be overlapping and do not have to be sequential.

_____ Using mini-lectures, evaluation sheets, information

DO-LOOK-LEARN 123

_____ papers, and the like to broaden and/or deepen the students' understanding of the task and the expected learnings.

_____ Giving the students opportunities to examine what happens as they do the tasks.

_____ Giving students opportunities to look at why these things happen, through a thoughtful examination.

_____ Giving students opportunities to make judgments about what happened as they did the tasks.

_____ Helping students think about how what they learned can be used for other, personally important situations in and out of the class setting.

_____ Checking to see if the objectives of the strategy have been met.

_____ Selecting new tasks that will follow up on what has been done and that are based on continuing feedback between students and the teacher.

SOME ADVANTAGES
The following are often mentioned as some of the advantages of the do-look-learn strategy:

- The strategy involves all students right from the start of a properly planned do-look-learn lesson.
- It is likely to cause all students to increase their awareness of how they work as individuals and as a group on a task.
- The method can be used effectively with slower students as well as with average and gifted students. For example, slower students may receive help from other members who are concerned with the growth of the group or from modeling their behavior along the lines of that of their peers. They may also mature in self-discipline and group skills from these contacts.
- The method can be used with varying age levels and in all the disciplines in the curriculum.
- It helps to increase motivation in students by allowing them to work with their friends in groups.
- The method is adaptable for developing all

aspects of learning: skills, understandings, and attitudes.
- The method is versatile for combining with other instructional strategies in learning; for example, *do* a simulation exercise for understanding the causes of the Civil War.

SOME DISADVANTAGES
The following are often mentioned as some of the disadvantages of the do-look-learn strategy:

- It is time-consuming in covering material, as compared with lecture, for example.
- It may require the teacher to spend an inordinate amount of time and energy preparing students for the *do* phase; the teacher may have to diversify the tasks, for example, so that students at different levels of readiness can succeed or at least cope.
- The method requires movable classroom furniture, as well as administrative support for non-traditional classroom structure and atmosphere, which may not be readily available.
- The strategy in its three stages may not be conducted adequately because of a rigid class schedule that limits necessary time and prevents follow-up.
- The strategy may be partially neglected in its *look* or *learn* stages because so much stress or interest may come from wanting to achieve a product or complete a task (the *do* stage). This might mean, for example, that concern with the process of *how* students are working and interacting becomes secondary or is eliminated.
- The name of the strategy may imply that the three stages are separate and sequential rather than possibly going on simultaneously or in a variety of orders, perhaps with repetition of stages. For example, the *look* could precede the *do*, if the teacher wished to establish a beginning for the lesson with regard to ways the students had been working previously. Another *look* could, of course, come again in the lesson.

CLASSROOM EXAMPLE (ELEMENTARY)
The special art teacher who visited an elementary school primary classroom during our observation came in with a cart of materials for the children to use in making mobiles of wire clothes hangers. She had an assortment of paper, several spools of thread, and a box of hole punches. She also had a few extra pairs of scissors for those children who might have misplaced theirs and a few extra clothes hangers for those who might have forgotten to bring these.

The regular classroom teacher reminded the children that it was time for art activities and asked them to put away all of the materials on which they had been working. The art teacher went to the round table in the center of the classroom area and began talking with the children.

"How many of you remembered to bring your clothes hangers today?" she asked. Several hands went up. She counted them and then counted the number of extra hangers that she had brought. She looked a bit concerned for a moment, and then explained to the children that although there were not enough hangers for everyone, they could work in small groups to learn how to make the mobiles. Then if they wanted to make mobiles on their own, they could do that later at home.

She asked each child to find a partner, because she had enough hangers for every two children in the class. When the children were settled next to their partners, the art teacher explained to them what the word *mobile* means. She showed them a sample mobile that had been made by a child in another class, and hung it on a hook at the front of the room. This mobile had multi-colored paper flowers hanging from it. She explained to the children that theirs could be any kind they wanted and that because they were working with someone else it could include a mixture of objects. Then she quickly cut out the shapes of a star and the moon, showed how holes could be made with the punch, attached thread through the holes, and tied the threads to the hanger so that the shapes dangled from it. She explained that it was necessary to balance the items on the hanger, so that the bottom cross bar would remain straight when the mobile was hung up.

After her demonstration, the art teacher

asked the students if they thought they were ready to begin. Most of them seemed eager to get started. She reminded them that if they had any difficulty making the mobile, she was available to help them.

The children began their work in pairs, with the teacher moving about the room supervising their work and answering questions. She also asked questions that she thought would help them in evaluating their progress. For example, she asked two partners who were having a difficult time deciding on what to cut out of the paper to explain their problem. One child said that they could not agree on what shapes they wanted to cut out. She reminded them of what she had said earlier: that the mobile could have several different things on it and that it was not necessary that they all be the same. The children decided they would each make different things and then cooperate in placing these on the mobile. Another pair was having difficulty using a punch—they kept getting the hole too close to the edge of the paper but could not see how to use the punch differently. The teacher asked one of them to show her how he was using the punch. When she saw the problem, she suggested that he use it a different way that worked better.

By this time, two speedy children had completed their mobile and were anxious to get the teacher's reaction to it. They brought it over for her to look at, and the teacher seemed very pleased with the results. She asked them how they had finished so quickly. They explained that they had decided what needed to be done and then split up the tasks. Concerned that this might mean they could not individually do complete mobiles on their own, the teacher asked each of them if he thought he had learned enough to do another one alone. Both said they thought they could. One of the pair said he thought he would try to do one at home that night to hang in his room. Because these two children had finished, the teacher asked them to assist her by going around the room and helping any of the other children who might be having difficulty learning how to make a mobile. She reminded them to help only if the children asked them to.

About five minutes before she was due to leave the classroom, the art teacher asked the children to begin putting away their materials in their desks and placing her materials on the cart. She suggested that those who had finished take their mobiles to the regular teacher who was now back in the room helping children hang the mobiles on a wire that had been permanently installed by the classroom windows for hanging art projects. She suggested that those who had not finished their mobiles try to complete them when there was a free time during the day.

The regular teacher thanked her colleague for planning such an interesting activity and commented on how well the children had learned to make mobiles in such a short time. The colorful mobiles that hung in the windows were proof of her statement.

Analysis/Comment (Elementary)

The art teacher was probably unaware that she was using the do-look-learn strategy in teaching the children how to make clothes-hanger mobiles. When she entered the classroom, her intent had been to give a brief lecture accompanied by a demonstration and then have the children work on their own. When they did not all have the necessary hangers, however, she decided to let them work in pairs and, in doing so, her work with the children took on an additional dimension. Working as pairs, the children were then forced to plan, produce, and evaluate their product along with another person in the class. In grouping them, she took one of the initial steps in using the do-look-learn strategy.

Grouping the children for the completion of a task, however, is only an initial step. If she had grouped the children and then supervised their work only by passing out materials as needed and assisting those who asked for help, then this example could not be considered do-look-learn. What she did do, however, was move about the room observing the children's progress and helping those who were having observable difficulties in looking at what was happening in their work and at what they might do to work better together. Some groups were thus involved in the *look* part of this method, as the teacher guided their thinking through problems they were having.

Because she was not intentionally using the do-look-learn strategy, however, some of the pairs probably did not analyze "what" was happening as they worked together and "why," as the strategy suggests they should. The teacher did talk with the pair that finished first about what each had "learned," in an effort to be certain that both of them really did learn how to make the mobile. She even asked them to help her in working with the other children, because both seemed confident that they now knew how to make the mobile. She did not go through the *learn* step with any other pair described in the example.

The teacher's time ran out, so she quickly supervised the cleaning up of the materials without an effective closing to this activity, which might have included a summary of what the children were now able to do differently because of the experience, and how these learnings could be used in other activities. She did not even comment on how well the class had done during the session.

Fortunately, the regular classroom teacher made a positive comment to the class, which undoubtedly made the children feel that it had been a successful experience in the eyes of their teacher.

This classroom example illustrates a point that we touch upon briefly in the introduction to this book. Many teachers use some of the strategies in a very natural way, without being fully aware that they are doing so. We believe, however, that with a greater awareness of their own behavior and a greater understanding of the strategy they may be using, they could use the strategy more effectively. Certainly this was true in the case of the special art teacher, whose plan for the day became a do-look-learn session when she found that she did not have enough clothes hangers for the project that she had planned.

CLASSROOM EXAMPLE (SECONDARY)

This illustration of do-look-learn strategy was observed during the teaching of an English class at the secondary level.

Previous and current work on poetry had made both the teacher and her ninth-grade class aware of the students' need for improving skills in interpersonal communication. During several periods with the class, the teacher developed—through classroom discussion aided by a hand-out—background knowledge regarding "communication" that all members could use as a kind of common data base. Students were encouraged to write, as best they could, a definition or example of the basic interpersonal communication skill: paraphrasing. They decided that paraphrasing is any means of showing another person what his idea or suggestion means to you, and they discussed how paraphrasing functions to improve clarity in one-to-one communication.

Few students could define or devise a paraphrase—and yet all claimed to see its value. With these facts in mind, the teacher chose the do-look-learn strategy to facilitate growth in paraphrasing. Shortly thereafter, when the students entered the classroom, the teacher grouped them into "helping trios." She required that each trio select from its members a helper, a helpee, and an observer. She then explained that the helper and the helpee were to talk about a problem that was real and important to the helpee (e.g., how to get a date for the Friday dance). A ground rule was that the helper could not offer ideas or suggestions until he had first paraphrased *to the satisfaction of the helpee* each major comment made by the helpee. A demonstration was given by the teacher to ensure understanding on this procedure.

The helper and helpee, now, had dual tasks: to interact toward solving a problem of the helpee, and—more especially for the helper—to work on using, consciously and deliberately, the skill of paraphrasing. The third member of each trio, the observer, was asked to look at the helper's performance: Did he seem to be listening? What, by the observed tally, was the total number of paraphrases he used? What were the key words of each? Can you identify the kind(s) of paraphrases used by the helper? (This last was an optional responsibility for the observer, dependent on his ability to use the hand-out received some days previously in class.)

The trios worked for approximately five minutes, until the teacher called a halt and asked the observer to share his observations with the helper and helpee. Then all three interacted, primarily on the helper's use of the skill of paraphrasing. They looked at how the application of the skill had affected their communication as well as at how it had contributed to solving the helpee's problem. The students rotated roles, and two more rounds, each about ten minutes, were completed. Between rounds, the teacher offered general feedback on the skill as she observed it being used during her supervision of the small groups. At the conclusion of the exercise, the class reviewed with the teacher the ways a paraphrase can be stated and the probable results from making use of paraphrases. Each student wrote a second definition and compared it with the one he had written earlier, noting changes in his personal understanding of paraphrasing.

It was then agreed to employ the skill of paraphrasing in future English classes in this unit. Use would be checked by the "stop-action" method, in which the teacher or designated students would ask the pupils to analyze the communication processess they had been using at the time they were asked to stop. Students selected for calling stop-actions would be those showing reasonable competence in paraphrasing. These students would be designated as teacher aides. Questions to be considered in the stop-action would include: Was the skill (paraphrasing) being used? If not, why not? Could and should it have been used? If it was being used, how was it affecting the interaction? Also, the teacher and class committed themselves to look, shortly, at some other skills and techniques related to interpersonal communication. Selection was to be based on student or teacher concerns, as these revealed a probable need.

With teachers and students on a reasonably similar wavelength regarding what they had been about in this do-look-learn lesson, and where they were going, class was dismissed.

Analysis/Comment (Secondary)
In the example cited, the three major operations of the do-look-learn method were rather clearly revealed. The teacher initiated her use of the strategy with a *do* phase which was really twofold: Students were to deal with an actual problem through a helping trio and to work on increasing individual competency in a communication skill, paraphrasing. Taking the beginning information at face value, the teacher has gathered sufficient evidence from past work by students to indicate to both herself and them that the decision to spend class time on such interpersonal communication skills as paraphrasing is appropriate. The inability of pupils to write an adequate definition of a paraphrase supports the validity of this decision.

The *look* stage becomes dominant when the students discuss with the observer the use of the skill; the helper, a role that each played before the exercise ended, was no doubt particularly alert at this time, because he was the major recipient of the feedback. The teacher's comments between rounds—in which she looked at how the class, on the whole, was working with paraphrasing—additionally helped students to look analytically at the skill under study. Although she made no clear effort to give students the opportunity to examine what happened and why it happened, or to make judgments about what happened, the teacher seemed to be at ease with the role of manager that she had set for herself. Assuming that she knows the full range of behavior associated with do-look-learn, her intention may well be to attend later to some of those checklist items seemingly skipped thus far. She may choose to do this when the students engage in the follow-up to which they have committed themselves.

The most evident *learn* in the example comes quite personally, through student comparison and assessment of the "before and after" written definitions and examples of paraphrasing. A measure of how much students learned—i.e., how capable they now seem to be with paraphrasing—could be compared with an instructional objective established earlier by the teacher. In the example cited, however, no such formal objective is apparent.

The *learn* phase is evident, again, through the discussion within each trio, especially after the observer's report. Students may come to understand, for instance, that one who wants to analyze his own skills of interpersonal communication can do so more accurately and completely with the help of others who are willing to provide feedback.

It might be conjectured that students are also likely to learn a better recognition of their roles in a helping trio experience from actually trying them out. Such learning improves the quality of subsequent helping trio exercises. One additional "spin-off" from this lesson could be the inclination of students to think about and look for paraphrasing in their family and out-of-school peer group interactions.

The teacher's announced intention to select qualified students as teacher aides will aid learning in the future. And, of course, the teacher can facilitate tie-ins among learning activities by consistently encouraging students to use skills of interpersonal communication; they could check out promises made by candidates for a school office by paraphrasing these, for example.

In all, the do-look-learn strategy seems to have been implemented in a fairly simple way in the classroom example provided. It did seem to be successful, if somewhat incomplete. The planned follow-up related to identified need would seem to be a logical time for both the teacher and the students to work through this important strategy more carefully.

NOTES

1. René Pino *et al.*, *Guide book for Program 151—Do-Look-Learn* (Portland, Ore.: Northwest Regional Educational Laboratory, 1969).

An Annotated List of Selected Resources for Further Study

STRATEGY 1: LECTURE

1. Callahan, Sterling G. *Successful Teaching in Secondary Schools.* Glenview, Ill.: Scott, Foresman and Co., 1971.

   Provides some helpful discussion on types of lectures and criteria for evaluating lectures, and offers examples of the lecture method in the classroom environment.

2. Colman, John E. *The Master Teachers and the Art of Teaching.* New York: Pitman Publishing Corp., 1967.

   Discusses, along with nineteen other approaches, the lecture method—its background, advantages, and disadvantages. Also reviews the five steps required in the formal lecture of today.

3. Hyman, Ronald T. *Ways of Teaching.* New York: J. B. Lippincott Co., 1970.

   Offers rationale, underlying justifications, and helpful guidelines to the lecture method as well as an example with commentary and variations on the lecture model.

4. Means, Richard. *Methodology in Education.* Columbus, Ohio: Charles E. Merrill Publishing Co., 1968.

   A little book with a lot (over 70) of "methods." It presents data on the lecture method and some versions of it—as lecture, discussion, outside speaker, indoctrination, and the like.

5. *Project English.* Washington, D.C.: United States Office of Education, 1966.

   These materials for K-12 English instruction, from the twenty-five federally funded curriculum study centers, offer a high degree of structure for the teacher. Some are at least partially built for the inclusion of the lecture technique and identify it as such.

STRATEGY 2: DISCUSSION

1. Glasser, William. *Schools Without Failure.* New York: Harper & Row, 1969.

   Among the most important innovations proposed by Dr. Glasser is the use of the class, led by the teacher, as a counseling group that daily spends time developing—through discussion—the social responsibility necessary to solve behavioral and educational problems within the class.

2. Gulley, Halbert E. *Discussion, Conference, and Group Process.* (2nd ed.) New York: Holt, Rinehart & Winston, 1968.

   A comprehensive textbook on discussion, this book promotes an understanding for teachers of the ways in which group discussion functions and how individuals become effective discussion leaders and participants. It emphasizes discussion for decision making and information sharing, and it also describes elements of public and large group discussion. The definitions, models, skills, evaluation measures, and overall ideas and information can be adapted for public school work and are useful for persons interested in teaching through the discussion strategy.

3. *Learning in the Small Group.* Melbourne, Fla.: Institute for Development of Educational Activities Information and Services Division (I/D/E/A/), P. O. Box 446, 32901, 1971.

A classroom manual based on a national seminar, this paperback illustrates and briefly describes twelve variations on learning in the small group. The presentations on structuring the small group are extremely valuable for beginning or experienced teachers who are interested in using the discussion strategy. A film based on the manual is also available. Both would be helpful in furthering understanding of the discovery strategy.

4. *The Fishbowl Design for Discussion.* Washington, D.C.: National Training Laboratories, 1812 K Street, N.W, 20006, 1970.

This exercise is one of a number of materials available through NTL to help teachers work with and through the discussion strategy. Its purposes are to help spread pupil participation and to increase student awareness of the roles played in a discussion.

5. *The Dynamics of Classroom Discussion.* Chicago: Great Books Foundation, 307 N. Michigan Avenue, 1970.

A twenty-hour course for classroom teachers in the discussion method of education. Designed for K-college teachers, it has application to every subject area in the curriculum and is geared to aiding discussion leaders develop skills and strategies for helping their students think and learn through discussion.

6. Stanford, Gene, and Barbara Dodds Stanford. *Learning Discussion Skills Through Games.* New York: Citation Press, 1969.

A small paperback that provides a sequence of skill-building games and activities designed to give students necessary practice in discussion techniques. It also presents fifteen remedial devices for use whenever a group shows signs of a particular weakness in working together.

7. Schmuck, Richard A., and Patricia A. Schmuck. *Group Processes in the Classroom.* Dubuque, Iowa: Wm. C. Brown Co., 1971.

The authors describe, through theory, research, and example, the basic characteristics of groups in the classroom. Very worthwhile in itself, this paperback is also an example of the many books available on "group processes"—activities that make use of the discussion strategy.

STRATEGY 3: DRILL AND PRACTICE

1. Allen, Dwight, and Eli Seifman (eds.). *The Teacher's Handbook.* Glenview, Ill.: Scott, Foresman and Co., 1971.

A reference book on many subjects in education, the *Handbook* offers information on using drill in mathematics, the psychology of drill, and some guidelines for viewing drill as a part of the learning process.

2. Conroy, Pat. *The Water Is Wide.* New York: Dell Publishing Co., 1972.

A serious, yet humorous, autobiography of one teacher's efforts to bring the black children of Yamacraw Island, South Carolina, into the twentieth century. Glimpses of a drill strategy are suggested, although—from an instructional strategy standpoint—the book more clearly offers an excellent real-life example of a teaching situation wherein drill would be appropriately employed for the benefit of the pupils. Very interesting reading!

3. Hoover, Kenneth. *Learning and Teaching in the Secondary School.* (3rd ed.) Boston: Allyn and Bacon, 1972.

In this representative "methods" text, the author offers a concise presentation of *practice* procedures in contrast with those of *review*. His instances of misuse of drill, the discussion of how repetitive practice contributes to skill acquisition, the illustrative lesson plan, and the guidelines for using drill—all contribute to a teacher's better understanding of the strategy.

4. Johnson, Clifton. *Old-Time Schools and School-Books.* New York: Dover Publications, 1963.

   A paperback that maps out American schooling from the Puritan days to the mid-nineteenth century. The many photographs, sketches, and materials represented and discussed remind the reader of the history of teaching in this country and its use of the drill and practice strategy, for better or for worse.

STRATEGY 4: INDEPENDENT STUDY

1. Alexander, William M., and Vynce A. Hines. *Independent Study in Secondary Schools.* New York: Holt, Rinehart & Winston, 1967.

   This book reports a survey aimed at defining and describing independent study practices as they existed in a sample of secondary schools in the school year of 1965-66. The survey was undertaken with the hope that the results would give some direction to future research and practice related to a highly important aim of secondary education, the development of the independent learner.

2. Beggs, David W. *Decatur-Lakeview High School: A Practical Application of the Trump Plan.* Englewood Cliffs, N. J.: Prentice-Hall, 1964.

   The story of how the staff of Lakeview High School in Decatur, Illinois, inaugurated a new organizational pattern for instruction based on large group and small group instruction and independent study. The plan was inspired by the writings of J. Lloyd Trump, as set forth in his book *Images of the Future.*

3. Beggs, David, and Edward G. Buffie (eds.). *Independent Study: Bold New Venture.* Bloomington: Indiana University Press, 1965.

   This collection of papers by researchers and practitioners deals with (1) the nature of independent study, (2) the goals of self-assumed learning activities, and (3) the way schools can organize to get independent study into the mainstream of the the school program. The articles were selected to help both elementary and secondary teachers.

4. Brown, B. Frank. *The Nongraded High School.* Englewood Cliffs, N. J.: Prentice-Hall, 1963.

   Chapter 5 explores independent study in the nongraded high school.

5. Gleason, Gerald T. (ed.). *The Theory and Nature of Independent Learning.* Scranton, Penn.: International Textbook Co., 1967.

   The conference from which these papers were taken explored independent learning from the viewpoints of learning research, motivational theory, socio-anthropological theory, and technological developments.

6. Trump, J. Lloyd, and Dorsey Baynham. *Guide to Better Schools.* Chicago: Rand McNally & Company, 1961.

   The study reported in this book was authorized by the National Association of Secondary School Principals' Commission on the Experimental School, and was financed by the Fund for the Advancement of Education and the Ford Foundation. The book reviews projects and experiments carried out in nearly 100 junior and senior high schools and designed to improve learning opportunities for students. A major thrust of many of these projects was the development of individual responsibility and skills of independent study.

STRATEGY 5: GROUP INVESTIGATION

1. Brown, Mary, and Norman Precious. *The Integrated Day in the Primary School.* New York: Agathon Press, 1968.

   Written by the headmaster of a junior school in Leicestershire and the headmistress of an associated infant school, this book describes their experiences in establishing an "integrated day" that involves small group investigation activities.

2. Bany, Mary A., and Lois V. Johnson. *Classroom Group Behavior: Group Dynamics in Education.* New York: Macmillan Co., 1964.

   The authors point out basic understandings related to the dynamic forces that affect the class as a group. Techniques for altering group behavior are included.

3. Causey, J. P., et. al. *Multi-Age Grouping: Enriching the Learning Environment.* Washington, D. C.: American Association of Elementary-Kindergarten-Nursery Educators, 1967.

   Written by a committee of Maryland educators, this booklet presents their case for multi-age grouping and describes ways in which it can enhance group investigation in an elementary school.

4. Napier, Rodney W., and M. K. Gershenfeld. *Groups: Theory and Experience.* Boston: Houghton-Mifflin Co., 1973.

   This handbook of group processes presents research findings and narrative accounts from the field which can be applied to classrooms at both the elementary and secondary level.

5. Nesbitt, Marion. *A Public School for Tomorrow.* New York: Dell Publishing Co., 1967.

   This book, originally published in 1953, describes the daily workings of the Matthew F. Maury School in Richmond, Virginia, as viewed by one of the teachers there. The principal and staff of the Maury School believed that the quality of living that students experience today determines in a large part their tomorrows and the tomorrows of the United States. In acting upon this belief, the staff involves the pupils in a variety of group experiences in all areas of the elementary school curriculum.

STRATEGY 6: LABORATORY APPROACH

1. Beechold, Henry F. *The Creative Classroom: Teaching Without Textbooks.* New York: Scribner, 1971.

   The author explores "think and do" activities related to life in contrast to the "read and memorize" process frequently used in school settings. He includes practical suggestions for classroom activity rather than focusing on school design or programing.

2. Brydegaard, Marguerite, and James Inskeep, Jr. *Mathematical Experiencing.* Washington, D. C.: American Association of Elementary-Kindergarten-Nursery Educators, 1972.

   This brief book reviews modern math practices and how to use the laboratory approach to teach mathematics to elementary school children.

3. Hooten, Joseph, and Michael Mahaffey. *Elementary Mathematics Laboratory Experiences.* Columbus, Ohio: Charles E. Merrill, 1972.

   Planned for the prospective teacher, this book explores ways of gaining proficiency with materials and techniques for using the laboratory approach in the teaching of elementary mathematics. The authors support the idea that through the use of concrete materials, the child and teacher gain deeper insights into the abstractness of mathematics.

4. Rice, Susan, and Rose Mukerji (eds.). *Children Are Centers for Understanding Media.* Washington, D. C.: Association for Childhood Education International, 1973.

   Published in collaboration with the Center for Understanding Media, this publication consists of fifteen articles dealing with techniques of teaching children to create their own media. Included are articles on child-produced still pictures, movies, photograms, slide mounts, flip-books, cut-out animations, story-boards, tape recordings, and transparencies. The authors reveal that involving children in the creation of media presents many possibilities for exciting learning experiences at home and at school.

5. Russell, Helen Ross. *Ten-Minute Field Trips: Using the School Grounds for Environmental Studies.* Chicago: J. G. Ferguson, 1973.

The author believes that the school grounds provide an always available natural laboratory for short field trips and that they are full of information about the environment, even if the school is surrounded by concrete and asphalt. This guidebook for teachers explores plants, animals, interdependence of living things, physical science, earth science, and ecology.

6. Wurman, Richard Saul (ed.). *Yellow Pages of Learning Resources.* Cambridge, Mass.: Group for Environmental Education (GEE!), MIT Press, 1972.

This book is modeled after the yellow pages of the telephone directory, with topics alphabetically listed from accountant to zoo. Each topic includes several ideas for learning activities that may take place at a particular place listed in the book. A chart points out that the suggestions are applicable for both big cities and small towns.

STRATEGY 7: DISCOVERY

1. Carin, Arthur A., and Robert B. Sund. *Developing Questioning Techniques: A Self-Concept Approach.* Columbus, Ohio: Charles E. Merrill Publishing Co., 1971.

This book presents practical suggestions for teachers in selecting, using, and evaluating appropriate questioning techniques. The stress throughout is on writing and using questions not only for assisting student cognitive achievement, but also as an aid in the building of student self-esteem and creativity.

2. *Effective Questioning: Elementary Level.* New York: Macmillan Co., 1968.

This four- to five-week mini-course package consists of color films and supporting materials to help teachers learn and reinforce specific skills that lead to active pupil involvement, higher thought processes, and a dramatic reduction in teacher talk in a classroom discussion. They would be very useful for pre-service and in-service teacher education.

3. *Facilitating Inquiry in the Classroom.* Portland, Ore.: Northwest Regional Educational Laboratory, 1973.

An instructional system based especially on the work of Dr. Richard Suchman, University of Illinois, these materials are designed to assist teachers develop and improve abilities in using 18 tactical moves that allow pupils to inquire. The system aids teachers in identifying what students do when they inquire and how they grow as inquirers. It also helps teachers diagnose and evaluate where individual students are on a continuum of inquirer growth. The system would be most appropriate for an in-service workshop of some forty-five hours of instruction on facilitating the inquiry process.

4. *Finding Out.* New York: Time/Life Films,.

A film that shows the methods by which a child can be made to discover things for himself in a "scientific" way.

5. Foster, John. *Discovery Learning in the Primary School.* Boston: Routledge & Kegan Paul, 1972.

A valuable study which deals with what is now recognized as the fundamental process in primary school education—discovery learning. The author discusses and analyses informal learning situations, examines the principles involved, and assesses the success of the methods and techniques used. The book is full of practical schemes, as well as discussion on the latest state of knowledge in the theory of discovery methods.

6. Hudgins, Bryce B. *The Instructional Process.* Chicago: Rand McNally & Co., 1971.

An interesting discussion and comparison of discovery learning in contrast with what the author terms "reception learning." In addition to describing part of the development of discovery techniques, this paperback lists the basic educational goals for the discovery strategy.

7. Hunkins, Francis P. *Questioning Strategies and Techniques.* Boston: Allyn & Bacon, 1972.

Devoted to helping teachers ask questions—a central behavior of the discovery strategy—

this paperback includes the major thinking of authorities such as Bloom, Suchman, and Taba. In addition, it offers the reader examples of types of questions at different levels of questioning and suggests various methods for evaluating the effectiveness of teacher-student question-asking behaviors.

8. Joyce, Bruce, and Marsha Weil. *Models of Teaching.* Englewood Cliffs, N. J.: Prentice-Hall, 1972.

   Presents a concept attainment model developed from a study of "discovery-type thinking" by Jerome S. Bruner and his associates. Its purpose is to teach students about the nature of concepts and the strategies people use to learn concepts.

9. McClosky, Mildred. *Teaching Strategies and Classroom Realities.* Englewood Cliffs, N. J.: Prentice-Hall, 1971.

   Offers fairly detailed classroom examples of discovery approaches attempted by teachers in the disciplines of English, science, mathematics, and social studies.

10. Michaelis, John U. *Social Studies for Children in a Democracy* (5th ed.). Englewood Cliffs, N. J.: Prentice-Hall, Inc., 1972.

    The central theme is that all children need to develop the thinking and inquiry processes essential for immediate and lifelong learning. With this goal in mind, the author brings together the best inquiry and conceptual approaches to social studies instruction. Chapters on "Developing Thinking and Inquiry Processes" and "Investigating Environmental Problems" are particularly relevant to the elementary school teacher who is interested in teaching through the discovery method.

11. Postman, Neil, and Charles Weingartner. *Teaching As a Subversive Activity.* New York: Delacorte Press, 1969.

    The authors see inquiry as a "survival strategy" needed by students. In an entertaining and thought-provoking style, they suggest teacher behaviors and attitudes to assist pupils in English and other disciplines in developing critical thinking abilities.

12. Raths, James, John R. Pancella, and James S. Van Ness. *Studying Teaching.* Englewood Cliffs, N. J.: Prentice-Hall, 1967.

    In a section on "Teaching Method," this text offers three articles directly related to discovery: one by Bruner on the act of discovery, one on teaching social studies through discovery, and one dealing with the rationale and mystique of the method.

13. Ryan, Frank L., and Arthur K. Ellis. *Instructional Implications of Inquiry.* Englewood Cliffs, N. J.: Prentice-Hall, 1974.

    Another addition to the rapidly growing number of inquiry-oriented texts and materials at all levels of instruction, this "methods" text defines inquiry in terms of specific operations applicable to classroom efforts of helping students, K-12, generate knowledge. Over sixty-five descriptions of classroom ideas for utilizing the content in a variety of curricular areas (especially social studies) are provided; in addition, the text assists prospective teachers in becoming actively involved in inquiry operations and, hence, in learning "inquiry" by becoming inquirers. The overall aim throughout the book is to establish an intimate and explicit tie between instructional theory and instructional practice.

14. Sanders, Norris M. *Classroom Questions: What Kinds.* New York: Harper & Row, 1966.

    A little book that classifies questions along the lines of Bloom's categories of thinking. The numerous examples and self-check "questions on questions" might be particularly useful to beginning teachers who are interested in expanding their question-asking repertoire.

15. Strasser, Ben B., *et. al. Teaching Toward Inquiry.* Washington, D. C.: National Education Association, 1971.

    Presented in an unusual format, this book is written as a resource for teachers. It deals with "why inquiry," "what people do as they inquire," "facilitating inquiry in the classroom," and "objectives in inquiry." Informative and interesting, it enables teachers to use discovery teaching in their classrooms.

STRATEGY 8: THE LEARNING CENTER

1. *Learning Centers: Children on Their Own.* Washington, D. C.: Association for Childhood Education International, 1970.

   A collection of articles by a variety of educators who support the learning center approach. Especially helpful is the section on "Evaluating and Recording Children's Activities: Diagnosing Educational Need." The illustrations are black-and-white photographs showing children working on their own in learning centers of different types.

2. Blackie, John. *Inside the Primary School.* London: Her Majesty's Stationery Office, 1967.

   A concise and well-written description of how the primary schools of England are organized today and what the children in them are learning. The author also tells how the schools and their present curriculum developed. He is the former Chief Inspector for Primary Education.

3. *Children Are People* (42-minute color film). New Gloucester, Me.: Leicestershire Learning Systems, Box 355.

   This film records the day-to-day experience of children working with each other and their teachers in mixed-age groupings in English infant and junior schools. Starting with the beginning 5-year-old entering the established environment of the family-grouped class, the film shows the development of relationships and learning processes within the informal atmosphere of the "integrated day" curriculum. Transitional stages and various combinations of flexible groupings up to 11 are explained by means of commentary and diagrams.

4. Forte, Imogene, and Joy Mackenzie. *Nooks, Crannies and Corners: Learning Centers for Creative Classrooms.* Nashville, Tenn.: Incentive Publications, 1972.

   Planned for teachers, administrators, and teachers-to-be, this is a handbook written by teachers for those in need of a simple, easy-to-follow outline and guide for developing and using learning centers. Examples are given for both primary and intermediate grades, and the "very practical appendix" includes space maps for arranging rooms, checklists for evaluating independent learning, and many other helpful ideas.

5. Franklin, Marian P. *Classroom Centers and Stations In America and Britain.* New York: MSS Information Corp., 1973.

   The author has selected 21 previously published accounts of how to get started with learning centers. Some of the articles describe how teachers have gradually moved into the use of this strategy. The book closes with an annotated list of 175 articles, books, and films on open education.

6. Godfrey, Lorraine. *Individualize with Learning Station Themes.* Menlo Park, Calif.: Individualized Books, 1974.

   Because learning centers are often easier to set up than to keep going, the author describes how a number of themes can be developed to provide both scope and continuity to the activities of a center.

7. *Open Classroom in America* (15-minute color film). Dayton, Ohio: I/D/E/A, 1972.

   Captures the teacher-child interactions, ranging from one-to-one relationships to large group situations which occur in the informal setting. The film shows the classroom areas where mathematics, language arts, science, handicrafts, and other specialized interests are pursued. The principal and teachers discuss the informal approach and what it means for students.

8. Sweeney, Connie, Mary Johnson, and Bobbie Bullard. *Centers Anyone?* Bloomington, Ind.: Phi Delta Kappa, 1974.

   This booklet was designed to assist the teacher with learning centers in the self-contained classroom. Included are suggestions for organizing materials, the classroom, scheduling of centers, levels of center growth, types of centers, center terminology, and center tracking sheets.

9. Voight, Ralph. *Invitation to Learning: the Learning Center Handbook.* Washington, D. C.: Acropolis Books, 1971.

   Presents a rationale for changing to a learning center approach, followed by specific ways in which a teacher can implement centers in an elementary or secondary classroom. Examples of a variety of centers, plus answers to some of the common questions raised by administrators, parents, and teachers are included.

10. William, Lois E. *Independent Learning . . . in the Elementary Classroom.* Washington, D. C.: American Association of Elementary-Kindergarten-Nursery Educators, 1969.

    Although the author emphasizes the learning center approach, she also presents a variety of ways in which independent learning skills can be developed. In discussing procedures for implementing programs for children that include independent learning, she places special emphasis on maintaining control, a concern expressed by many teachers moving into independent learning activities.

STRATEGY 9: SIMULATION

1. Adams, Dennis M. *Simulation Games: An Approach to Learning.* Worthington, Ohio: Charles A. Jones Publishing Co., 1973.

   Written for the teacher, this book translates simulation theory into practice and presents guidelines for understanding, designing, constructing, and using simulation games. An extensive sampling of simulation games available on the commercial market is included.

2. "Teaching About Spaceship Earth: A Role-Playing Experience for the Middle Grades," *Intercom* No. 71. New York: Center for War/Peace Studies of the New York Friends Group, 218 East 18 St., 1972; also available by special arrangement from the Association for Childhood Education International, Washington, D. C.

   This issue of *Intercom* is directed to elementary teachers. The first section presents research into attitude formation in children, and the second section describes in detail a role-playing simulation situation suitable for middle-grade children.

3. Gillies, Emily. *Creative Dramatics for All Children.* Washington, D. C.: Association for Childhood Education International, 1973.

   The author presents guidelines for deepening children's sense-awareness and expressiveness.

4. Mandell, Muriel. *Games to Learn By.* New York: Sterling Publishing Co., 1972.

   Originally published in 1958 under the title *101 Best Educational Games*, this book includes chapters entitled "Ice-breakers," "Music, Art, and Puppetry Games," "Nature Study and Science Games," "Language Arts Games," "Mathematical Games," and "Social Science Games." The games have been sequenced by degree of difficulty within each chapter.

5. *A Mask for Me, A Mask for You* (16-minute color film). New York: Universal Educational and Visual Arts.

   A "rejected" child discovers identity and satisfaction through creative expression and role playing. The film emphasizes the enjoyment and fulfillment a child can experience through such activities.

6. Shaftel, Fannie R., and George Shaftel. *Role Playing for Social Values.* Englewood Cliffs, N. J.: Prentice-Hall, 1967.

   The authors present forty-seven stories valuable for helping children explore and develop values through role playing.

7. Zuckerman, David W., and Robert E. Horn. *The Guide to Simulation Games for Education and Training.* Cambridge, Mass.: Information Resources, 1970.

   A comprehensive list of games and simulations that are currently available for classroom application is included in this helpful publication.

STRATEGY 10: BEHAVIOR MODIFICATION

1. Ackerman, J. Mark. *Operant Conditioning Techniques for the Classroom Teacher.* Glenview, Ill.: Scott, Foresman and Co., 1972.

   A practical guide that offers many suggestions for preventing disruptive behavior and encouraging growth in learning. Of particular value is the section entitled "Preparing a Master Plan for Behavior Change." The author believes the techniques described in his book are most readily applied to changing the behavior of children between kindergarten and grade six.

2. *Conversation with B. F. Skinner* (20-minute color film). Del Mar, Calif.: CRM Educational Films, 1972.

   The noted behaviorist discusses the origin of behaviorism and some of its basic principles. He also describes some of the problems involved in implementing behavior modification systems in both open and closed settings.

3. Haring, Norris, and E. Lakin Phillips. *Analysis and Modification of Classroom Behavior.* Englewood Cliffs, N. J.: Prentice-Hall, 1972.

   Designed for pre-service and in-service teachers who wish to learn about behavior modification and to acquire skills in the use of this strategy. The book includes a thorough treatment of the foundational concepts of conditioning, a description of numerous research studies on behavior modification, examples and case studies of classroom use of behavior modification, and an examination of the parents' role in behavior modification.

4. Krumboltz, John D., and Helen B. Krumboltz. *Changing Children's Behavior.* Englewood Cliffs, N. J.: Prentice-Hall, 1972.

   The authors present what they believe to be a common-sense way to correct behavior problems using the new concepts of psychological research. They present more than 150 examples of how these concepts are applied to a variety of problems, from fear of the dark to fighting in the classroom. These examples are reinforced with illustrations from *Seventeen* magazine, the Peanuts and Dennis the Menace cartoon strips, and other relevant sources.

5. Madsen, Charles H., and Clifford K. Madsen. *Teaching Discipline: Behavioral Principles Toward a Positive Approach.* Boston: Allyn and Bacon, 1970.

   This brief and readable book presents specific classroom situations in which behavior modification principles can be used. Suggested responses for teachers to make in these situations are also included.

6. O'Leary, K. D., and S. G. O'Leary (eds.). *Classroom Management: The Successful Use of Behavior Modification.* New York: Pergamon Press, 1972.

   This book of readings presents the behaviorist's approach to modifying children's classroom reactions. Its purpose is to "supply the reader with a set of principles in historical context of the development of treatment with children." Choosing natural rewards, wise use of school service personnel, difficulties involved in the definition of abnormality, and other topics are discussed. The focus is on what works in the classroom.

7. Poteet, James A. *Behavior Modification: A Practical Guide for Teachers.* Minneapolis, Minn.: Burgess Publishing Co., 1973.

   This brief guide takes the newcomer to behavior modification through the following stages: describing, measuring, understanding, modifying, and evaluating behavior and behavior changes.

8. Sulzer, Beth, and G. Roy Mayer. *Behavior Modification Procedures for School Personnel.* Dryden Press, 1972.

   Written for educators and others concerned with the development of children, this is a guidebook to the study of behavioral technology. Behavioral science as a discipline is considered in relation to the individual and the circumstances surrounding behavior modification.

9. Thoresen, Carl E. (ed.). *Behavior Modification in Education*, 72nd Yearbook. Chic-

ago: National Society for the Study of Education, 1973.

Written by many of the leading figures in the behavior modification movement, the purpose of this book is (1) to provide a perspective on the historical and contempory development of behavior modification, (2) to analyze and synthesize the work on this subject as it relates to educational theory, (3) to stimulate inquiry by professional educators as to the applicability of behavior modification in educational practice, (4) to identify and deal with the issues of behavior modification as they relate to education, and (5) to broaden professional perspectives of educational decision-makers concerning behavior modification.

STRATEGY 11: PERFORMANCE—BASED LEARNING ACTIVITY PACKAGES

1. Davies, Ivor K. *Competency Based Learning: Technology, Management, and Design.* New York: McGraw-Hill, 1973.

    A comprehensive book oriented more to the secondary school teacher than to the elementary teacher. Overall, it deals with the management of learning, while each chapter offers more precise objectives on such performance strategy items as writing objectives, measuring learning, and moving toward a technology of education and training.

2. Duke, Charles R. "A Learning Activity Package: Discovering Dialects," the *English Journal*, March 1973, pp. 432-40.

    Here is an illustrative package geared to performance-based instruction. Especially helpful for teachers of English in grades 9-12, it exemplifies the sequence and organization that go into making LAP's for pupil use. With a little adaption, this LAP could be taught by teachers interested in getting a "feel" for teaching through the PBLAP strategy.

3. Houston, W. Robert. *Exploring Competency Based Education*, Berkeley, Calif.: McCutchan Publishing Corp., 1974.

    Written by leaders in the competency movement, the book speculates on the meaning of CBE, considers some of the major issues involved in its implementation, outlines several alternative design processes, considers the basic dimensions of assessment and evaluation, and examines fundamental notions of the institutional change process. A comprehensive 700-item bibliography includes published and unpublished papers, modules, books, and research studies related to CBE.

4. Leonard, Leo D., and Robert T. Utz. *Building Skills for Competency Based Teaching.* New York: Harper & Row, 1974.

    One of the very few texts now on the market that systematically presents the basic skills needed to develop a competency-based curriculum. The general characteristics of performance-based education are explained and basic skills needed for curriculum building are presented along the lines, for example, of applying learning concepts, considering taxonomies of educational objectives, and evaluation. Each chapter contains behavioral objectives and self-evaluation activities.

5. *Mini-Catalog of Instructional Systems.* Washington, D. C.: Technological Applications Project, U. S. Department of Health, Education and Welfare, Office of Education, 1974.

    Lists the descriptive course titles and sources of more than 175 systems that have been successfully programed and implemented for independent study in various schools throughout the country. All levels and academic areas are represented.

6. Nagel, Thomas S., and Paul T. Richman. *Competency-Based Instruction: A Strategy to Eliminate Failure.* Columbus, Ohio: Charles E. Merrill Publishing Co., 1972.

    A branching-programed text that helps the pre-service or in-service K-12 teacher gain a clear and concise statement of what competency-based instruction is and what its value, parameters, and methods of operation should be. The sample modules and flow charts are especially helpful to teachers planning to implement the PBLAP strategy.

7. Popham, W. James, and Eva L. Baker. *Establishing Instructional Goals; Planning*

an Instructional Sequence; Classroom Instructional Tactics; Evaluating Instruction. Englewood Cliffs, N. J.: Prentice-Hall, 1970, 1973.

This series of programed paperbacks focuses—as the titles suggest—on some crucial topics related to competency-based instruction. The texts could help teachers establish a "readiness" for working with the PBLAP strategy.

8. Weigand, James (ed.). *Developing Teacher Competencies*, Englewood Cliffs, N. J.: Prentice-Hall, 1971.

A self-instructional programed text. Contains field-tested material prepared by experts in areas central to the PBLAP strategy. Teachers could use the text, for example, to develop their skills in formulating performance objectives, developing question-asking skills, and developing competency for sequencing instruction.

STRATEGY 12: DO-LOOK-LEARN

1. Borton, Terry. *Reach, Touch and Teach.* New York: McGraw-Hill, 1970.

   The "what—so what—now what" approach described here, like the "do-look-learn" that parallels it, can be applied for learning processes and for dealing with a variety of content. For example, one can learn if he *does* paraphrase, or *how to* paraphrase, or if he *has* paraphrased accurately a certain problem, thus providing for all concerned (at least in part) a measure of one's learning—whether it be in communication, math, history, a personal concern, or whatever. In all, this is a useful reference for persons who are interested in building a curriculum in which student concerns are paramount, and the kind of instructional methods represented by "do-look-learn" and "what—so what—now what" are prime components.

2. Gorman, Alfred H. *Teachers and Learners: The Interactive Process of Education.* (2nd ed.). Boston: Allyn & Bacon, 1974.

   The basic assumption in this paperback is that teaching with learning involves a process of communication among individuals in a group setting. The reference undergirds the "do-look-learn" type of instruction by providing a description of important content and process behaviors, interaction exercises, and, perhaps most helpfully, a number of data-gathering instruments that are extremely useful for aiding students and teachers to "look" at themselves and their learnings.

3. Greer, Mary, and Bonnie Rubinstein. *Will the Real Teacher Please Stand Up?* Pacific Palisades, Calif.: Goodyear Publishing Co., 1972.

   A kind of "Whole-Earth Catalog" for educators, this delightful and worthwhile paperback offers numerous specific tasks that could be rather easily adapted for the *do* and *look* components of the "do-look-learn" method. Moreover, process and product learning are likely to be facilitated by the quality and inherent interest of the tasks made available by the authors.

4. Johnson, David W. *Reaching Out.* Englewood Cliffs, N. J.: Prentice-Hall, 1972.

   An excellent source of theory and experiences that are necessary to help individuals take a look at themselves and the effectiveness of their interpersonal relationships! The many exercises are geared to "do-look-learn" instruction, with emphasis on analyzing, for personal growth, one's process of communication and on building each learner's repertoire of skills for interpersonal communication.

5. Jung, Charles, René Pino, *et. al. Interpersonal Communications.* Portland, Ore.: Office of Program 100 Field Relations and Dissemination, Northwest Regional Educational Laboratory, 1971.

   An instructional package of twenty units built to give teachers knowlege and skills generally applicable to the transfer of meaning on a one-to-one basis. The units provide competencies in such specific skills as "paraphrasing," "identifying the effects of feelings on communication," and "applying guidelines to giving and receiving feedback." Materials used in the units are developed on a "do-look-learn" basis. Additional programs for teachers' growth are available from the Laboratory. These also reflect the "do-look-learn" strategy.

6. Simon, Sidney, Leland Howe, and Howard Kirschenbaum. *Values Clarification: A Handbook of Practical Strategies for Teachers and Students.* New York: Hart Publishing Co., 1972.

This paperback describes 79 "strategies" for aiding in the processes of choosing, acting on, and prizing one's beliefs and behaviors. The "Procedure" sections in the standardized format parallel the *do* of "do-look-learn"; some of the "Purpose" provides information relevant to what to learn, and experience with the activities helps students focus on "looking" at their own values and those of others.